Editor
Eric Migliaccio

Managing Editor
Ina Massler Levin, M.A.

Editor-in-Chief
Sharon Coan, M.S. Ed.

Illustrator
Howard Chaney

Cover Artist
Lesley Palmer

Art Coordinator
Kevin Barnes

Art Director
CJae Froshay

Imaging
Ralph Olmedo, Jr.
Rosa C. See

Product Manager
Phil Garcia

Portions used under license from *The World Almanac for Kids*. Copyright (c) 2003 World Almanac Education Group, Inc. All Rights Reserved.

Publishers
Rachelle Cracchiolo, M.S. Ed.
Mary Dupuy Smith, M.S. Ed.

THE WORLD ALMANAC FOR KIDS

BRAIN TEASERS
Book 2

Grades 3-4

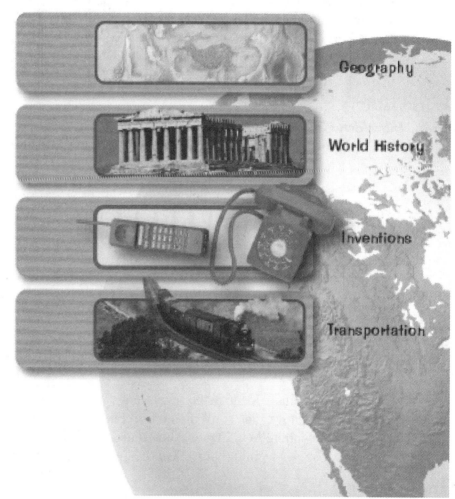

Geography

World History

Inventions

Transportation

Author

Melissa Hart

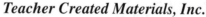

Teacher Created Materials, Inc.
6421 Industry Way
Westminster, CA 92683
www.teachercreated.com

ISBN-0-7439-3786-4

©2003 Teacher Created Materials, Inc.

Made in U.S.A.

Table of Contents

Introduction

The World Almanac for Kids Brain Teasers combines the educational benefits of the information-rich *The World Almanac for Kids* with the fun and challenges of brain teasers. While the brain teasers in this book vary in difficulty level, they are geared towards children in grades 3 and 4. Chockfull of information from *The World Almanac for Kids*, these puzzles and games will provide hours of stimulating activities for children. The wide assortment of brain teasers utilize a variety of skills, providing enjoyment for all types of learners.

How to Use *The World Almanac for Kids Brain Teasers*

The World Almanac for Kids Brain Teasers is divided into sections by subject. Within each section there are several introductory pages followed by many pages of brain teasers.

✻ Introductory Pages

The introductory pages provide valuable information on the subject. For instance, at the beginning of the section on Geography, you will find information about each of the seven continents, as well as a list of many of the explorers who discovered these lands. Much of the information that will be needed to solve the brain teasers is included in this section. Be sure to discuss or read these pages with your class to ensure that they have the appropriate background knowledge. You may wish to have your students solve the brain teasers in conjunction with these introductory pages, or you may wish to have them do the brain teasers using other resources.

✻ Brain Teasers

Within each section there are games, puzzles, and activities that are designed to be both educational and entertaining. Each brain teaser can stand alone as a quick filler activity or used to reinforce a unit of study.

You may wish to have your students solve the brain teasers with partners, especially when you are introducing brain teasers or if you believe the particular activity will be challenging to your class. Working with partners or in small groups allows each child to draw on the knowledge and strengths of classmates as well as display his or her own knowledge and strengths. This will prevent frustration and keep the activities enjoyable.

The activities in this book utilize students' multiple intelligences. The brain teasers are designed to help develop the following:

    ✗ critical-thinking skills   ✗ creative-thinking skills

    ✗ research skills   ✗ spelling skills

    ✗ vocabulary skills   ✗ math skills

    ✗ memory skills   ✗ visual-spatial skills

# Geography

Almost two-thirds of Earth's surface is made up of water. The rest is land. The largest areas of water are called oceans, and the biggest pieces of land are called continents. There are four oceans and seven continents on Earth:

THE FOUR OCEANS

The facts about the oceans include their size and average depth.

PACIFIC OCEAN: 64,186,300 square miles; 12,925 feet deep

ATLANTIC OCEAN: 33,420,000 square miles; 11,730 feet deep

INDIAN OCEAN: 28,350,500 square miles; 12,598 feet deep

ARCTIC OCEAN: 5,105,700 square miles; 3,407 feet deep

Let's take a close look at the seven continents:

	Area	2001 Population	Highest Point	Lowest Point
North America	8,300,000 square miles	486,000,000	Mount McKinley (Alaska), 20,320 feet	Death Valley (California), 282 feet below sea level
South America	6,800,000 square miles	351,000,000	Mount Aconcagua (Argentina), 22,834 feet	Valdes Peninsula (Argentina), 131 feet below sea level
Europe	8,800,000 square miles	729,000,000	Mount Elbrus (Russia), 18,510 feet	Caspian Sea (Russia, Azerbaijan; eastern Europe and western Asia), 92 feet below sea level
Asia	12,000,000 square miles	3,737,000,000	Mount Everest (Nepal, Tibet), 29,035 feet	Dead Sea (Israel, Jordan), 1,312 feet below sea level
Africa	11,500,000 square miles	823,000,000	Mount Kilimanjaro (Tanzania), 19,340 feet	Lake Assal (Djibouti), 512 feet below sea level
Australia & Oceania	3,200,000 square miles	31,000,000	Mount Kosciusko (New South Wales), 7,310 feet	Lake Eyre (South Australia), 52 feet below sea level
Antarctica	5,400,000 square miles	No permanent residents	Vinson Massif, 16,864 feet	Bentley Subglacial Trench, 8,327 feet below sea level

The deepest part of any ocean is the Marianas Trench, located just west of the Philippines in the Pacific Ocean. Its depth is 35,840 feet—almost 7 miles. That's greater than the height of the tallest mountain on Earth!

Here are a few of the longest, tallest, etc., things on Earth.

- **Longest River:** Nile, in Egypt & Sudan (4,160 miles)
- **Highest Waterfall:** Angel Falls, in Venezuela (3,212 feet)
- **Tallest Mountain:** Mount Everest, in Tibet & Nepal (29,035 feet)
- **Biggest Lake:** Caspian Sea, in Europe & Asia (143,244 sq. mi.)

- **Biggest Desert:** The Sahara, in Africa (3,500,000 square miles)
- **Biggest Island:** Greenland, in the Atlantic Ocean (840,000 square miles)
- **Deepest Cave:** Lamprechtsofen-Vogelschacht, in Salzburg, Austria (5,354 feet deep)

The world is a huge place with all kinds of places to go and things to see. These days, you can go on the Internet and see pictures of far-away places. Imagine how it used to be long ago, though, when no one knew what lay on the other side of a mountain or ocean. The following people were some of the explorers who braved the unknown in order to make the world a little less mysterious.

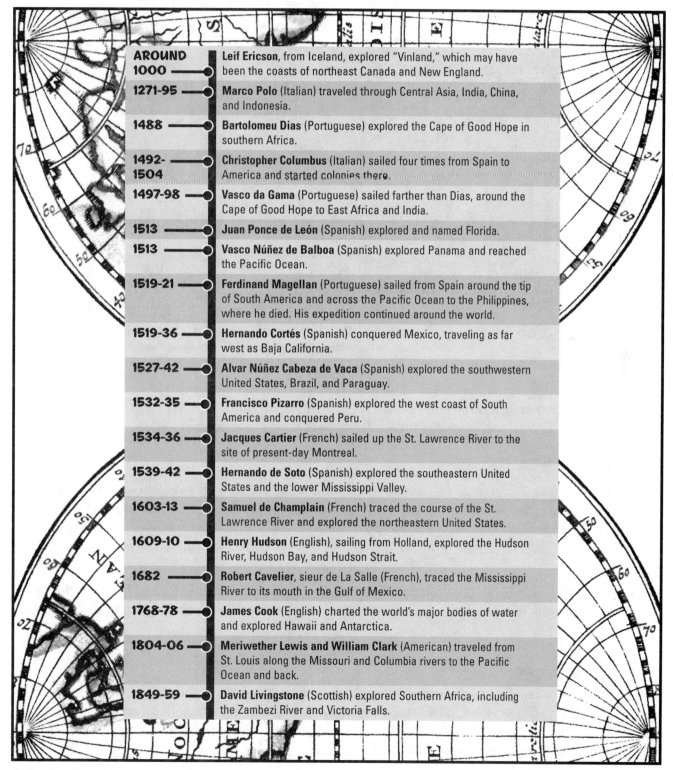

AROUND 1000	**Leif Ericson**, from Iceland, explored "Vinland," which may have been the coasts of northeast Canada and New England.
1271-95	**Marco Polo** (Italian) traveled through Central Asia, India, China, and Indonesia.
1488	**Bartolomeu Dias** (Portuguese) explored the Cape of Good Hope in southern Africa.
1492-1504	**Christopher Columbus** (Italian) sailed four times from Spain to America and started colonies there.
1497-98	**Vasco da Gama** (Portuguese) sailed farther than Dias, around the Cape of Good Hope to East Africa and India.
1513	**Juan Ponce de León** (Spanish) explored and named Florida.
1513	**Vasco Núñez de Balboa** (Spanish) explored Panama and reached the Pacific Ocean.
1519-21	**Ferdinand Magellan** (Portuguese) sailed from Spain around the tip of South America and across the Pacific Ocean to the Philippines, where he died. His expedition continued around the world.
1519-36	**Hernando Cortés** (Spanish) conquered Mexico, traveling as far west as Baja California.
1527-42	**Alvar Núñez Cabeza de Vaca** (Spanish) explored the southwestern United States, Brazil, and Paraguay.
1532-35	**Francisco Pizarro** (Spanish) explored the west coast of South America and conquered Peru.
1534-36	**Jacques Cartier** (French) sailed up the St. Lawrence River to the site of present-day Montreal.
1539-42	**Hernando de Soto** (Spanish) explored the southeastern United States and the lower Mississippi Valley.
1603-13	**Samuel de Champlain** (French) traced the course of the St. Lawrence River and explored the northeastern United States.
1609-10	**Henry Hudson** (English), sailing from Holland, explored the Hudson River, Hudson Bay, and Hudson Strait.
1682	**Robert Cavelier**, sieur de La Salle (French), traced the Mississippi River to its mouth in the Gulf of Mexico.
1768-78	**James Cook** (English) charted the world's major bodies of water and explored Hawaii and Antarctica.
1804-06	**Meriwether Lewis and William Clark** (American) traveled from St. Louis along the Missouri and Columbia rivers to the Pacific Ocean and back.
1849-59	**David Livingstone** (Scottish) explored Southern Africa, including the Zambezi River and Victoria Falls.

Below is a map of an imaginary place. Could you find your way around if you went there?

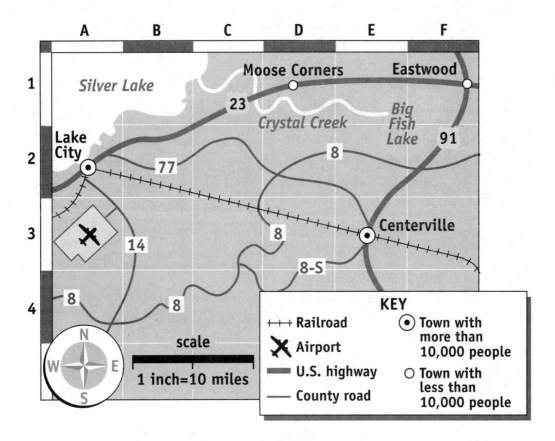

DIRECTION

Maps usually have a **compass rose** that shows you which way is north. On most maps, like this one, north is straight up. When north is up, south is down, east is right, and west is left.

DISTANCE

Of course the distances on a map are much shorter than the distances in the real world. The **scale** shows you how to estimate the real distance. In the map above, every inch on paper stands for a real distance of 10 miles.

PICTURES

Maps usually have little pictures or symbols. The map **key** tells what they mean. Take a look at the key above. Which are the two smallest cities on the map? How would you get from the airport to Centerville by car?

FINDING PLACES

Many maps have a list of places in alphabetical order, with a letter and number for each. In the map above, you can find Centerville (E3) by drawing a straight line down from the letter E on top, and another line going across from the number 3 on the side. Lines made like this form a **grid**. Centerville should be near the place on the grid where the lines for E and 3 meet.

Did you ever travel on a spaceship? In a way, you're traveling around the Sun right now on a spaceship called Planet Earth.

THINKING GLOBAL

A globe is a small model of Earth. Like Earth, it is shaped like a ball or sphere. Earth isn't exactly a sphere because it gets flat at the top and bottom and bulges a little in the middle. This shape is called an **oblate spheroid.**

Because Earth is round, most flat maps that are centered on the equator do not show the shapes of the land masses exactly right. The shapes at the top and bottom usually look too big. For example, the island of Greenland, which is next to North America, may look bigger than Australia, though it is really much smaller.

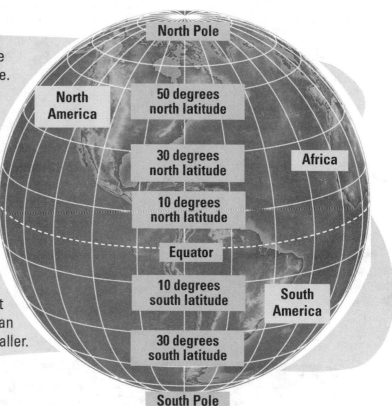

LATITUDE AND LONGITUDE

Imaginary lines that run east and west around Earth, parallel to the equator, are called **parallels**. They tell you the **latitude** of a place, or how far it is from the equator. The equator is at 0 degrees latitude. As you go farther north or south, the latitude increases. The North Pole is at 90 degrees north latitude. The South Pole is at 90 degrees south latitude.

Imaginary lines that run north and south around the globe, from one pole to the other, are called **meridians**. They tell you the degree of **longitude**, or how far east or west a place is from an imaginary line called the Greenwich meridian or prime meridian (0 degrees). That line runs through the city of Greenwich in England.

Which Hemispheres Do You Live In?

Draw an imaginary line around the middle of Earth. This is the **equator**. It splits Earth into two halves called **hemispheres**. The part north of the equator, including North America, is the northern hemisphere. The part south of the equator is the southern hemisphere.

You can also divide Earth into east and west. North and South America are in the western hemisphere. Africa, Asia, and most of Europe are in the eastern hemisphere.

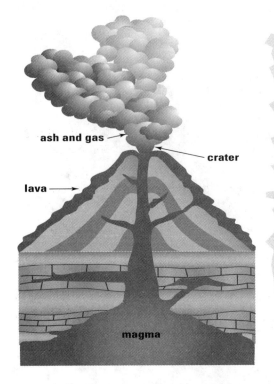

ash and gas

crater

lava

magma

A volcano is a mountain or hill with an opening on top known as a **crater**. Hot melted rock (**magma**), gases, ash, and other material from inside the earth mix together a few miles underground, rising up through cracks and weak spots in the mountain. Every once in a while, the mixture may blast out, or erupt, through the crater. The magma is called **lava** when it reaches the air. This red-hot lava may have a temperature of more than 2,000 degrees Fahrenheit. The hill or mountain is made of lava and other materials that come out of the opening, and then cool off and harden.

Some islands are really the tops of undersea volcanoes. The Hawaiian islands developed when volcanoes erupted under the Pacific Ocean.

SOME FAMOUS VOLCANIC ERUPTIONS		
Year	Volcano (place)	Deaths (approximate)
79	Mount Vesuvius (Italy)	16,000
1586	Kelut (Indonesia)	10,000
1792	Mount Unzen (Japan)	14,500
1815	Tambora (Indonesia)	10,000
1883	Krakatau or Krakatoa (Indonesia)	36,000
1902	Mount Pelée (Martinique)	28,000
1980	Mount St. Helens (U.S.)	57
1982	El Chichón (Mexico)	1,880
1985	Nevado del Ruiz (Colombia)	23,000
1986	Lake Nyos (Cameroon)	1,700
1991	Mt. Pinatubo (Philippines)	800

WHAT CAUSES EARTHQUAKES? The Earth's outer layer, its **crust**, is divided into huge pieces called **plates**. These plates, made of rock, are constantly moving—away from each other, toward each other, or past each other. A crack in Earth's crust between two plates is called a **fault**. Many earthquakes occur along faults where two plates collide as they move toward each other or grind together as they move past each other. Earthquakes along the **San Andreas Fault** in California are caused by the grinding of two plates.

MEASURING EARTHQUAKES The Richter scale (see below) goes from 0 to more than 8. These numbers indicate the strength of an earthquake. Each number means the quake releases about 30 times more energy than the number below it. An earthquake measuring 6 on the scale is about 30 times stronger than one measuring 5 and 900 times stronger than one measuring 4. Earthquakes that are 4 or above are considered major. (The damage and injuries caused by a quake also depend on other things, such as whether the area is heavily populated and developed.) The strength of an earthquake is registered on an instrument called a **seismograph** and is given a number on a scale called the **Richter scale**.

MAGNITUDE	EFFECTS
0–2	Earthquake is recorded by instruments but is not felt by people.
2–3	Earthquake is felt slightly by a few people.
3–4	People feel tremors. Hanging objects, like ceiling lights, swing.
4–5	Earthquake causes some damage; walls crack; dishes and windows may break.
5–6	Furniture moves; earthquake seriously damages weak buildings.
6–7	Furniture may overturn; strong buildings are damaged; walls and buildings may collapse.
7–8	Many buildings are destroyed; underground pipes break; wide cracks appear in the ground.
Above 8	Total devastation, including buildings and bridges; ground wavy.

Unscramble the following words to reveal the names of the seven highest points on the continents. You may use the word bank for help.

1. **tuMon imilKanoraj**

   _____

2. **noutM eilckMny**

   _____

3. **noMut Kookssuic**

   _____

4. **osnniV safMis**

   _____

5. **Muton sblEur**

   _____

6. **nutMo agacAnuoc**

   _____

7. **unotM sEertve**

   _____

Word Bank

Mount Aconcagua   Vinson Massif

Mount Elbrus   Mount McKinley

Mount Everest   Mount Kilimanjaro

Mount Kosciusko

Use the clues below to fill in the puzzle and to find out about some the biggest and most amazing things on Earth.

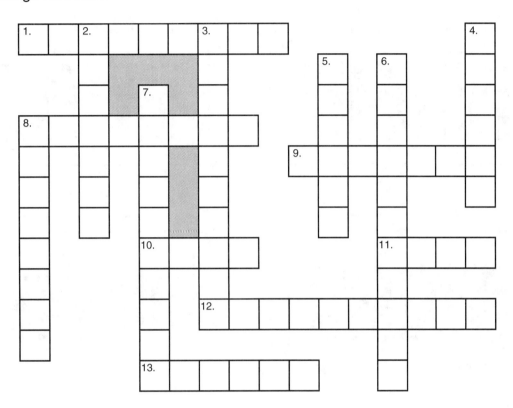

Across

1. What is the name of the biggest island on Earth?
8. This trench is the deepest and lowest spot on Earth.
9. At over 64,000,000 square miles, this is our biggest ocean.
10. More people live on this continent than on the other six combined.
11. The longest river in the world is the _____.
12. And the highest waterfall is _____.
13. It's easily the smallest of the four oceans.

Down

2. This mountain is the highest on Earth.
3. This continent is the least populated. In fact, no one calls this place home for too long.
4. The longest river, the Nile, winds its way through this continent.
5. At about 3,500 square miles, this is the largest desert.
6. This mountain is the largest in Africa.
7. Though we call it a sea, this body of water is officially the largest lake on Earth.
8. Up in Alaska, we can find this mountain, the highest in North America.

A car license plate can tell something about its owner. Decode these plates to reveal clues to the names of famous explorers.

1.
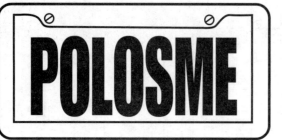
POLOSME

_____

2.

CHRISCO

_____

3.

JPDLEON

_____

4.

COOKH2O

_____

5.
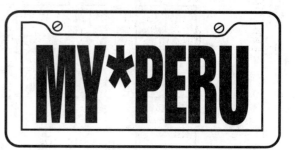
MY*PERU

_____

6.

HOPE4ME

_____

7.

HHSAILS

_____

8.

MEXI4ME

_____

Read these clues about explorers. Write a name in each blank to complete the chart. You may use the name bank below for help.

Nationality	Discovery	Name
1. Spanish	southeastern United States	
2. Portuguese	across Pacific Ocean to the Philippines	
3. French	St. Lawrence River to Montreal	
4. Scottish	Southern Africa	
5. British	Hawaii and Antarctica	
6. Spanish	Panama and the Pacific Ocean	
7. Italian	Central Asia, India, China, Indonesia	
8. American	Missouri and Columbia Rivers to Pacific Ocean	
9. Icelandic	Canada and New England	
10. Spanish	South America and Peru	

Name Bank

Marco Polo   Meriweather Lewis and William Clark

Leif Ericson   Francisco Pizarro

Hernando de Soto   Ferdinand Magellan

Jacques Cartier   Vasco Núñez de Balboa

David Livingstone   James Cook

The names of explorers have been split into two- or three-letter pieces. The letters of the pieces are in order, but the pieces are scrambled. Put the letters together to identify the explorers. Use the clues and the name bank to help you.

1. RO BE ER VE LI RT CA

   ⇒ French explorer _____

2. HE AN ES RN RT DO CO

   ⇒ traveled west to Baja California _____

3. JU ON EDE AN PO LE NC

   Spanish explorer _____

4. BA OM AS DI EU RT OL

   ⇒ explored Africa _____

5. CH LU RI ER CO STO MB US PH

   ⇒ started colonies _____

6. IN MU DEC SA HA EL LA MP

   ⇒ explored the United States _____

7. HE DS HU NRY ON

   ⇒ sailed from Holland _____

8. JA UES RTI CQ CA ER

   ⇒ explored Canada _____

9. FR ANC RO CO ZAR IS PI

   ⇒ Spanish explorer _____

10. FE ND GEL INA MA RD LAN

   ⇒ Died during his expedition _____

Name Bank

Ferdinand Magellan	Juan Ponce de León
Jacques Cartier	Christopher Columbus
Bartolomeu Dias	Samuel de Champlain
Henry Hudson	Robert Cavelier
Francisco Pizarro	Hernando Cortés

Solve the clues and place the proper nouns in the puzzle below. Some of the letters have been provided for you.

1. I sailed around the tip of South America and across the Pacific Ocean.

2. I conquered Mexico in the 16th century.

3. I am a group of islands first explored by James Cook around the 1770s. Later, I became the 50th U.S. state.

4. I sailed along the St. Lawrence river into what is now Montreal.

5. I traveled into the lower Mississippi Valley in 1539. Who am I?

6. I reached the Pacific Ocean in 1513.

7. I explored Victoria Falls in Southern Africa during the mid-19th century.

8. I am an Englishman who sailed from Holland into what is now Canada.

9. I traveled southwest from Iceland around 1000 B.C. to explore. Who am I?

10. I am an Italian who traveled extensively through Central and Southeastern Asia during the 13th century.

11. I explored and named Florida. Which European country did I call home?

12. I traced the Mississippi River to its mouth in the Gulf of Mexico. Which European country did I call home?

13. I explored Antarctica in the 18th century.

Use this compass and the map of the continental United States on page 17 to answer the questions below.

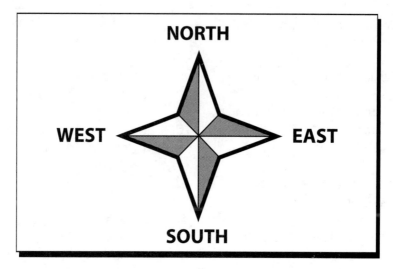

1. Where would you be if you traveled one state north of California?

_____

2. Where would you be if you traveled two states south of Nebraska?

_____

3. Where would you be if you traveled two states south of Washington?

_____

4. Where would you be if you traveled one state east of Idaho?

_____

5. Where would you be if you traveled one state north of New Mexico?

_____

6. Where would you be if you traveled two states west of Colorado?

_____

7. Where would you be if you traveled one state north of Texas?

_____

8. Where would you be if you traveled one state south of Georgia?

_____

9. Where would you be if you traveled two states east of Mississippi?

_____

10. Where would you be if you traveled one state east of Colorado?

_____

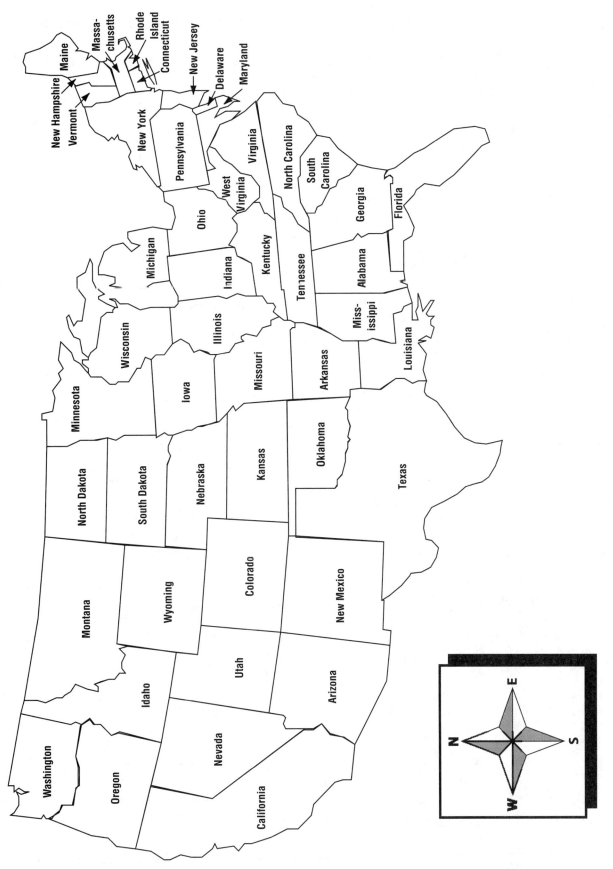

Use the map key and the map below to answer the questions.

1. Near what city would you find an airport? _____

2. What type of road would you take to get from Lake City to Moose Corners?

   _____

3. In what town could you find less than 10,000 people? _____

4. What kind of road would you take to get from Lake City to Mowmouth?

   _____

5. Through what two cities does the train travel?_____

6. What three cities have more than 10,000 people? _____

7. What type of road would you take to get from Centerville to Eastwood?

   _____

8. Where is Mowmouth in relation to Lake City (north, south, east, or west)?

   _____

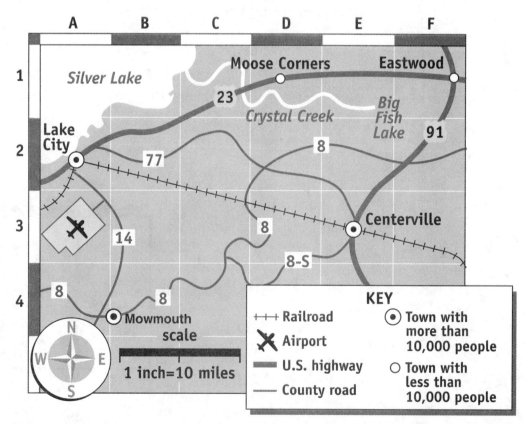

Study the cross-section of the globe below. The equator and some of the latitudes are marked. Answer the questions below.

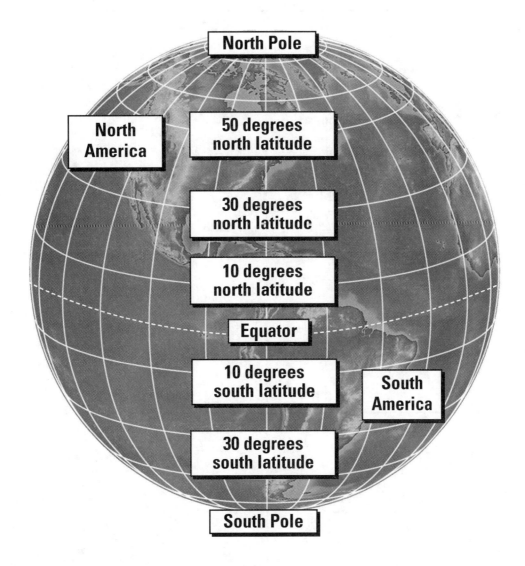

1. What continent would you be in at the equator? _____

2. Which Pole would be at 90° north? _____

3. What continent is at 45° north? _____

4. Where would you be at 30° south? _____

5. What continent is at 50° north? _____

6. Where would you be at 90° south? _____

Using the globes below, decide whether each country is in the Northern or Southern Hemisphere. Check **North** or **South**. The equator is labeled on each globe.

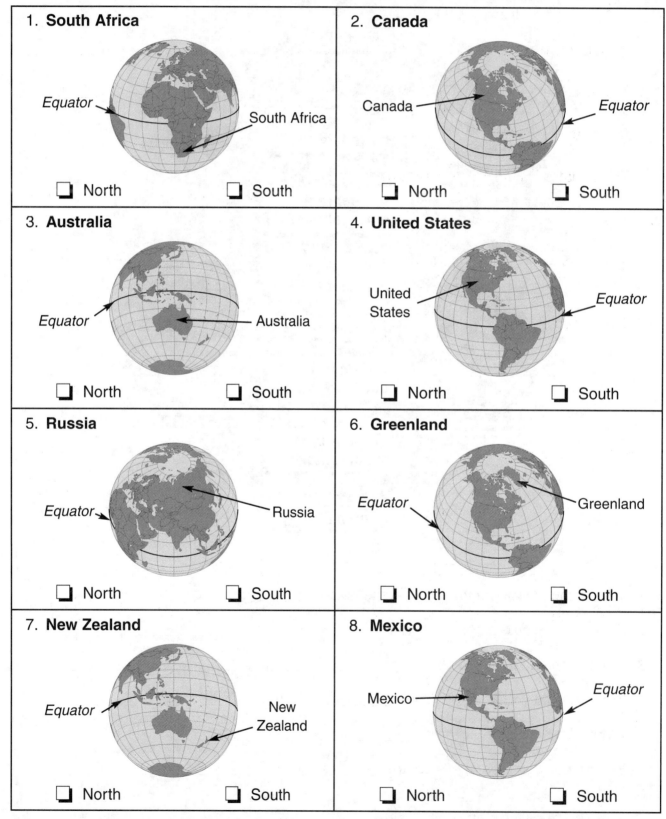

1. **South Africa**

Equator

South Africa

☐ North ☐ South

2. **Canada**

Canada

Equator

☐ North ☐ South

3. **Australia**

Equator

Australia

☐ North ☐ South

4. **United States**

United States

Equator

☐ North ☐ South

5. **Russia**

Equator

Russia

☐ North ☐ South

6. **Greenland**

Equator

Greenland

☐ North ☐ South

7. **New Zealand**

Equator

New Zealand

☐ North ☐ South

8. **Mexico**

Mexico

Equator

☐ North ☐ South

Fill in the blanks and fit the answers into the puzzle spaces below.

1. The _____ is at 90° north latitude.

2. Imaginary lines that run parallel to the equator are called _____.

3. The imaginary line around the middle of the earth is called the _____.

4. North America is in the _____ hemisphere.

5. The equator splits the earth into two halves called _____.

6. The _____ is at 90° south latitude.

7. Imaginary lines that run north and south, from one pole to the other, are called _____.

8. The Greenwich meridian runs through the city of Greenwich in _____.

Fill in the crossword puzzle by answering the clues below.

Across

2. ocean in which volcanoes erupted and formed the Hawaiian Islands

6. hot melted rock, gases, and ash

7. a mountain with an opening on top

8. this describes the temperature of lava as it spills out

Down

1. what magma becomes when it reaches the air

3. the tops of some undersea volcanoes

4. the opening on top of a volcano

5. what the volcano does when the magma inside gets very hot

Unscramble the words below to reveal famous volcanic eruptions. You may use the word bank for help.

1. teluK

   _____

2. toMun leePe

   _____

3. raTboam

   _____

4. aLke syNo

   _____

5. tM batouniP

   _____

6. lE hiochnC

   _____

7. otMun nUzne

   _____

8. ukatraKa

   _____

9. utoMn usuVesiv

   _____

10. tonuM tS leensH

   _____

Word Bank

Mount Pelée	Mount St. Helens
Krakatau	Mount Unzen
Kelut	Mt. Pinatubo
Lake Nyos	El Chichón
Mount Vesuvius	Tambora

Match the famous volcano to its location. Some answers will be used more than once.

_____ 1. El Chichón

_____ 2. Lake Nyos

_____ 3. Mount St. Helens

_____ 4. Kelut

_____ 5. Navado del Ruiz

_____ 6. Mount Vesuvius

_____ 7. Tambora

_____ 8. Mt. Pinatubo

_____ 9. Krakatau

_____ 10. Mount Pelée

_____ 11. Mount Unzen

a. Indonesia

b. U.S.

c. Japan

d. Martinique

e. Cameroon

f. Philippines

g. Mexico

h. Columbia

i. Italy

Solve these mysteries with names of famous volcanoes. Study the clues, and use page 8 as a reference.

1. I killed 1,700 people in 1986.

   ⟹ Who done it? _____

2. I erupted in ancient Italy.

   ⟹ Who done it? _____

3. I blew my top in the United States in 1980.

   ⟹ Who done it? _____

4. I'm responsible for more deaths than any other volcano, way back in 1883.

   ⟹ Who done it? _____

5. I erupted in Japan over two hundred years ago.

   ⟹ Who done it? _____

6. Mexico wasn't glad to see me in 1982.

   ⟹ Who done it? _____

7. I was the first of three major volcanoes in Indonesia.

   ⟹ Who done it? _____

8. I killed 800 people in the Philippines, not long ago.

   ⟹ Who done it? _____

Read the effects of each earthquake on the chart below. Fill in the appropriate Richter scale magnitude.

MAGNITUDE	EFFECTS
0–2	Earthquake is recorded by instruments but is not felt by people.
2–3	Earthquake is felt slightly by a few people.
3–4	People feel tremors. Hanging objects, like ceiling lights, swing.
4–5	Earthquake causes some damage; walls crack; dishes and windows may break.
5–6	Furniture moves; earthquake seriously damages weak buildings.
6–7	Furniture may overturn; strong buildings are damaged; walls and buildings may collapse.
7–8	Many buildings are destroyed; underground pipes break; wide cracks appear in the ground.
ABOVE 8	Total devastation, including buildings and bridges; ground wavy.

1. The couch slides across the room, and the shed out back falls down.

   ➠ What is the magnitude? _____

2. Water and gas pipes break, and the street shows huge cracks.

   ➠ What is the magnitude? _____

3. Instruments record it, but no one feels it.

   ➠ What is the magnitude? _____

4. Walls crack, and a window breaks.

   ➠ What is the magnitude? _____

5. Buildings and bridges collapse, and there is total ruin.

   ➠ What is the magnitude? _____

6. A wall collapses, and the dresser overturns.

   ➠ What is the magnitude? _____

7. The ceiling lights swing, and you feel the ground shake.

   ➠ What is the magnitude? _____

8. A few people feel it.

   ➠ What is the magnitude? _____

Fill in the sentences below, and then locate the underlined words in the word search. Words may go up, down, or horizontally. Use the word bank below for help.

1. The earth's outer layer is called its _____.

2. The San Andreas Fault is found in _____.

3. A _____ is a crack in the earth's crust between two plates

4. A huge piece of the earth's crust is called a _____.

5. When two plates collide, there is an _____.

6. The earth's plates are made of _____.

7. The earth's plates are constantly _____.

8. The ground _____ during an earthquake.

c	f	a	h	e	d	g	s	g	h	c	o	s	k	e	d	s	k	o	g
g	a	g	h	k	o	e	d	k	j	r	e	o	w	l	d	h	k	e	d
p	u	b	m	e	d	i	g	u	e	u	p	l	a	t	e	a	l	m	d
o	l	w	l	k	n	g	i	o	e	s	w	c	k	d	i	k	q	i	e
b	t	w	d	g	i	e	e	a	r	t	h	q	u	a	k	e	g	h	i
j	x	z	c	m	d	k	o	e	c	l	w	p	w	d	d	s	l	o	p
c	a	l	i	f	o	r	n	i	a	w	p	l	e	m	g	d	o	p	s
b	s	o	p	d	v	v	w	p	d	l	k	b	o	d	s	j	o	p	w
w	o	p	d	m	g	o	i	s	g	p	i	n	d	s	i	n	p	g	s
w	o	p	s	g	k	b	s	n	w	g	s	o	i	n	r	o	c	k	s
q	w	u	i	r	o	x	d	m	g	b	s	p	o	i	n	g	s	i	t

Word Bank

moving	plate
fault	shakes
earthquake	crust
rock	California

Shake it Up!

Use the letters in the phrase, "Shake, Rattle, and Roll" to answer the clues below.

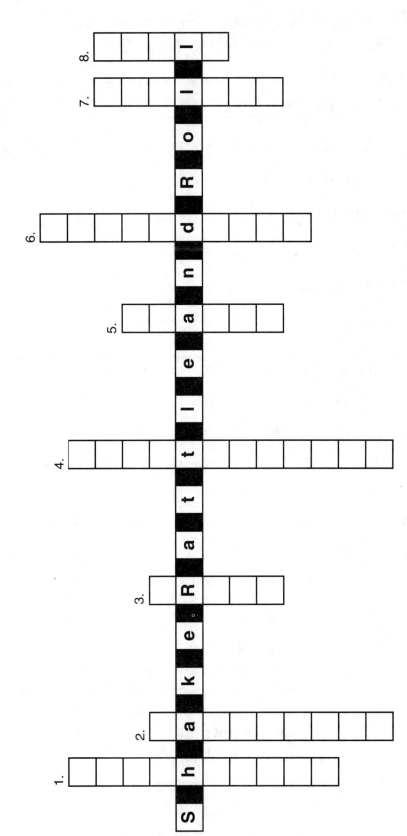

Clues

1. what happens when two plates collide or grind together
2. The strength of an earthquake is called this.
3. This outer layer is divided into huge pieces.
4. This scale is used to measure an earthquake.
5. huge pieces of the Earth's crust
6. a fault in California, caused by the grinding of two plates
7. what plates do during an earthquake
8. a crack in the Earth's crust between two plates

The ancient Greeks worshipped gods who they believed lived on Mount Olympus. The Romans had similar gods, but with different names. Here is a list of some of those gods and their unique traits.

GREEK NAME	ROMAN NAME	KNOWN AS
Zeus	Jupiter	All-powerful king of the gods. Used a lightning bolt to strike down wrongdoers.
Hera	Juno	Zeus's wife and sister. Angered Zeus by playing favorites with mortals.
Poseidon	Neptune	Zeus's brother and god of the sea. He could unleash storms. Sailors prayed to him for a safe voyage.
Hades	Pluto	Zeus's brother, god of the underworld, where the dead lived as ghostly shadows.
Athena	Minerva	Zeus's daughter, goddess of wisdom. Scholars, soldiers, and craftsmen prayed to her for sharp wits.
Aphrodite	Venus	Goddess of love. She could make people fall in love. Using this skill against other gods made her powerful.
Hephaestus	Vulcan	Son of Zeus and Hera, god of craftsmen and blacksmiths. Ugly and lame, he could work magic with a hammer and anvil.
Apollo	none	Zeus's son and god of the sun, medicine, poetry, and music. Every day, Apollo drove his golden chariot (the Sun) across the sky. He was handsome, coolheaded, and fierce in battle.
Artemis	Diana	Apollo's twin sister, goddess of the moon and the hunt. She punished those who killed animals unnecessarily.

Algeria

Antigua and Barbuda

Australia

Bangladesh

Brazil

Canada

Fiji

Gabon

The Gambia

Georgia

Germany

Ghana

Greece

Grenada

Guinea

Guinea-Bissau

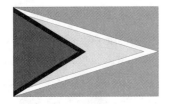

Guyana

Japan

Kazakhstan

Lebanon

Macedonia

Malaysia

Maldives

Mauritania

Namibia

Netherlands

New Zealand

Pakistan

Palau

Peru

San Marino

Singapore

Somalia

Turkey

Tuvalu

United Kingdom

Uzbekistan

Venezuela

Vietnam

Zimbabwe

THE ANCIENT MIDDLE EAST

4000–3000 B.C.
► The world's first cities are built by the Sumerian peoples in Mesopotamia, now southern Iraq.
► Sumerians develop a kind of writing called cuneiform.
► Egyptians develop a kind of writing called hieroglyphics.

2700 B.C. Egyptians begin building the great pyramids in the desert. The pharaohs' (kings') bodies are buried in them.

1792 B.C. Some of the first written laws are created in Babylonia. They are called the Code of Hammurabi.

ACHIEVEMENTS OF THE ANCIENT MIDDLE EAST

Early peoples of the Middle East:

1 Studied the stars (astronomy).

2 Invented the wheel.

3 Created written language from picture drawings (hieroglyphics and cuneiform).

4 Established the 24-hour day.

5 Studied medicine and mathematics.

1200 B.C. Hebrew people settle in Canaan in Palestine after escaping from slavery in Egypt. They are led by the prophet Moses.

THE TEN COMMANDMENTS

Unlike most early peoples in the Middle East, the Hebrews believed in only one God (monotheism). They believed that God gave Moses the Ten Commandments on Mount Sinai when they fled Egypt.

1000 B.C. King David unites the Hebrews in one strong kingdom.

ANCIENT PALESTINE Palestine was invaded by many different peoples after 1000 B.C., including the Babylonians, the Egyptians, the Persians, and the Romans. It came under Arab Muslim control in the 600s and remained mainly under Muslim control until the 1900s.

336 B.C. Alexander the Great, King of Macedonia, builds an empire from Egypt to India.

63 B.C. Romans conquer Palestine and make it part of their empire.

AROUND 4 B.C. Jesus Christ, the founder of the Christian religion, is born in Bethlehem. He is crucified about A.D. 29.

ANCIENT AFRICA

ANCIENT AFRICA In ancient times, northern Africa was dominated, for the most part, by the Egyptians, Greeks, and Romans. However, we know very little about the lives of ancient people in Africa south of the Sahara Desert (sub-Saharan Africa).

The people of Africa south of the Sahara did not have written languages in ancient times. What we learn about them comes from such things as weapons, tools, and other items from their civilization that have been found in the earth.

2000 B.C. The Kingdom of Kush arises just south of Egypt. It becomes a major center of art, learning, and trade. Kush dies out around A.D. 350.

500 B.C. The Nok culture becomes strong in Nigeria, in West Africa. The Nok use iron for tools and weapons. They are also known for their fine terra-cotta sculptures of heads.

AROUND A.D. 1 Bantu-speaking peoples in West Africa begin to move into eastern and southern Africa.

50 The Kingdom of Axum in northern Ethiopia, founded by traders from Arabia, becomes a wealthy trading center for ivory.

300s Ghana, the first known African state south of the Sahara Desert, takes power in the upper Senegal and Niger river region. It controls the trade in gold that is being sent from the southern parts of Africa north to the Mediterranean Sea.

660s–900 The Islamic religion spreads across North Africa and into Spain.

ANCIENT EUROPE

4000 B.C. People in many parts of Europe start building monuments out of large stones called megaliths. Examples can still be seen today, including Stonehenge in England.

2500 B.C.–1200 B.C.

1 People on the island of Crete (Minoans) in the Mediterranean Sea built great palaces and became sailors and traders.

2 People in the city of Mycenae in Greece built stone walls and a great palace.

3 Mycenaean people invaded Crete and destroyed the power of the Minoans.

THE TROJAN WAR The Trojan War was a conflict between invading Greeks and the people of Troas (Troy) in Southwestern Turkey around 1200 B.C. Although little is known today about the real war, it has become a part of Greek poetry and mythology. According to a famous legend, a group of Greek soldiers hid inside a huge wooden horse. The horse was pulled into the city of Troy. Then the soldiers jumped out of the horse and conquered Troy.

900-600 B.C. Celtic peoples in Northern Europe settle on farms and in villages and learn to mine for iron ore.

600 B.C. Etruscan peoples take over most of Italy. They build many cities and become traders.

SOME ACHIEVEMENTS OF THE GREEKS

The early Greeks were responsible for:

1 The first governments that were elected by people. Greeks invented democratic government.

2 Great poets such as Homer, who composed the *Iliad*, a long poem about the Trojan War, and the *Odyssey*, an epic poem about the travels of Odysseus.

3 Great thinkers such as Socrates, Plato, and Aristotle.

4 Great architecture, like the Parthenon and the Propylaea on the Acropolis in Athens.

431 B.C. The Peloponnesian Wars begin between the Greek cities of Athens and Sparta. The wars end in 404 B.C. when Sparta wins.

338 B.C. King Philip II of Macedonia in northern Greece conquers all the cities of Greece.

336 B.C. Philip's son Alexander becomes king. He conquers lands and makes an empire from the Mediterranean Sea to India. He is known as Alexander the Great. For the next 300 years, Greek culture dominates this vast area.

ANCIENT ASIA

3500 B.C. Communities of people settle in the Indus River Valley of India and Pakistan and the Yellow River Valley of China.

2500 B.C. Cities of Mohenjo-Daro and Harappa in Pakistan become centers of trade and farming.

AROUND 1523 B.C. Shang peoples in China build walled towns and use a kind of writing based on pictures. This writing develops into the writing Chinese people use today.

1500 B.C. The Hindu religion (Hinduism) begins to spread throughout India.

AROUND 1050 B.C. Chou peoples in China overthrow the Shang and control large territories.

700 B.C. In China, a 500-year period begins in which many warring states fight one another.

563 B.C. Siddhartha Gautama is born in India. He becomes known as the Buddha—which means the "Enlightened One"—and is the founder of the Buddhist religion (Buddhism).

551 B.C. The Chinese philosopher Confucius is born. His teachings—especially the rules about how people should treat each other—spread throughout China and are still followed today.

TWO IMPORTANT ASIAN RELIGIONS Many religions began in Asia. Two of the most important were:

Hinduism. Hinduism began in India and has spread to other parts of southern Asia and to parts of the Pacific region.

Buddhism. Buddhism also began in India and spread to China, Japan, and Southeast Asia. Today, both religions have millions of followers all over the world.

320-232 B.C.: INDIA Northern India is united under the emperor Chandragupta Maurya. Also, Asoka, emperor of India, sends Buddhist missionaries througout southern Asia to spread the Buddhist religion.

221 B.C. The Chinese ruler Shih Huang Ti makes the Chinese language the same throughout the country. Around the same time, the Chinese begin building the Great Wall of China. Its main section is more than 2,000 miles long and is meant to keep invading peoples from the north out of China.

202 B.C. The Han people of China win control of all of China.

ACHIEVEMENTS OF THE ANCIENT CHINESE

1 Invented paper.

2 Invented gunpowder.

3 Studied astronomy.

4 Studied engineering.

5 Invented acupuncture to treat illnesses.

THE AMERICAS

10,000-8000 B.C. People in North and South America gather plants for food and hunt animals using stone-pointed spears.

AROUND 3000 B.C. People in Central America begin farming, growing corn and beans for food.

1500 B.C. Mayan people in Central America begin to live in small villages.

500 B.C. People in North America begin to hunt buffalo to use for meat and for clothing.

100 B.C. The city of Teotihuacán is founded in Mexico. It becomes the center of a huge empire extending from central Mexico to Guatemala. Teotihuacán contains many large pyramids and temples.

A.D. 150 Mayan people in Guatemala build many centers for religious ceremonies. They create a calendar and learn mathematics and astronomy.

900 Toltec warriors in Mexico begin to invade lands of Mayan people. Mayans leave their old cities and move to the Yucatan Peninsula of Mexico.

1000 Native Americans in the southwestern United States begin to live in settlements called pueblos. They learn to farm.

1325 Mexican Indians known as Aztecs create huge city of Tenochtitlán and rule a large empire in Mexico. They are warriors who practice human sacrifice.

1492 Christopher Columbus sails from Europe across the Atlantic Ocean and lands in the Bahamas, in the Caribbean Sea. This marked the first step toward the founding of European settlements in the Americas.

1500 Portuguese explorers reach Brazil and claim it for Portugal.

1519 Spanish conqueror Hernándo Cortés travels into the Aztec Empire in search of gold. The Aztecs are defeated in 1521 by Cortés. The Spanish take control of Mexico.

WHY DID THE SPANISH WIN? How did the Spanish defeat the powerful Aztec Empire in such a short time? One reason is that the Spanish had better weapons. Another is that the Aztecs became sick and died from diseases brought to the New World by the Spanish. The Aztecs had never had these illnesses before and, as a result, did not have immunity to them. Also, many neighboring Indians hated the Aztecs as conquerors. Those Indians helped the Spanish to defeat them.

1534 Jacques Cartier of France explores Canada.

1583 The first English colony in Canada is set up in Newfoundland.

1607 English colonists led by Captain John Smith settle in Jamestown, Virginia. Virginia was the oldest of the Thirteen Colonies that eventually became the United States.

1619 First African slaves arrive in English-controlled America.

1682 The French explorer Robert Cavelier, sieur de la Salle, sails down the Mississippi River. The area is named Louisiana after the French King Louis XIV.

Have you ever wondered what life was like 100 years ago? Look at the information below to find out what was going on in the years 1903 and 1904.

100 YEARS AGO—1903

► Bicycle riders raced 1,500 miles across France's countryside, as the now-famous Tour de France was held for the first time.

► In the first World Series, the Boston Pilgrims upset the Pittsburgh Pirates, five games to three.

► Orville Wright took off on a 12-second, 120-foot flight at Kitty Hawk, North Carolina, the first successful airplane flight in history.

► The silent film *The Great Train Robbery* became the first major American movie. It was also the first movie with a realistic plot.

► Mary Harris Jones led hundreds of workers, including children, in a 100-mile march from Philadelphia to New York to protest their long hours of work in mills and factories.

► Pierre and Marie Curie shared the Nobel Prize in Physics for their work with radioactive elements, including two that they had discovered (radium and polonium).

100 YEARS AGO—1904

► The New York City subway system opened. This system grew to become the biggest in the U.S., and one of the largest in the world.

► Denton True "Cy" Young became the first player in major league history to pitch a perfect game, allowing no batter to reach first base.

► The first comic books were published; they were collections of popular cartoons and comic strips that had already appeared in newspapers.

► The first Olympic Games in the United States were held in the summer in St. Louis, Missouri. They were part of the World Exposition celebrating the 100th anniversary of the Louisiana Purchase.

► Helen Keller, who was both blind and deaf, graduated from Radcliffe College; she had already written a famous book, *The Story of My Life* (1902).

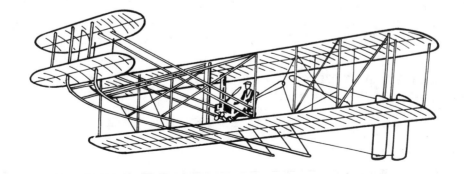

Study the list of the world's flags on pages 30 and 31. Then answer the following questions.

1. Name three countries that start with a **G**._____

   _____

2. Which flag is decorated with a picture of a tree? _____

3. Which flag is decorated with a leaf? _____

4. Name three flags that have crescent moons on them._____

   _____

5. What two flags are decorated with a single star?_____

   _____

6. What three flags are decorated only with a single circle? _____

   _____

7. What country begins with a **Z**? _____

8. Name the four flags that are decorated with some form of the Union Jack (the flag of the United Kingdom).

   _____

   _____

   _____

9. What country has the same name as a U.S. state? _____

10. Name two flags that are decorated with a sun. _____

    _____

Complete this puzzle by cutting out the individual pieces to form a flag belonging to one of our world's nations. To what country does this flag belong?

_____
(country)

Match the Greek god or goddess with his/her description.

_____ 1. Zeus

_____ 2. Hera

_____ 3. Poseidon

_____ 4. Hades

_____ 5. Athena

_____ 6. Aphrodite

_____ 7. Hephaestus

_____ 8. Apollo

_____ 9. Artemis

a. I'm the goddess of wisdom—people pray to me before tests.

b. My brother is king, and he lets me rule over the underworld.

c. I make my husband angry because I like some humans better than others.

d. I may not be good-looking, but you should see me use my hammer and anvil!

e. I'm the god of the sea—be nice to me, or I'll send down a storm.

f. I've got a golden set of wheels that I drive across the sky every day.

g. My brother is god of the sun. I am goddess of the moon, and I protect the animals.

h. I'm a king who rules with my lightning bolt.

i. I can make you fall in love with whomever I choose!

Use the chart on gods and goddesses to match the Roman god or goddess with his or her description below.

_____ 1. Jupiter

_____ 2. Juno

_____ 3. Neptune

_____ 4. Pluto

_____ 5. Minerva

_____ 6. Venus

_____ 7. Vulcan

_____ 8. Diana

A. I'm the goddess of wisdom; scholars pray to me before tests.

B. My brother is king, and he lets me rule over the underworld.

C. I make my husband angry because I like some mortals better than others.

D. I may not be good-looking, but you should see me use my hammer and anvil!

E. I'm the god of the sea—be nice to me, or I'll send down a storm.

F. I'm the king who rules with my lightning bolt.

G. My brother is god of the sun. I am goddess of the moon, and I protect the animals.

H. I can make you fall in love with whomever I choose!

Many of the Greek and Roman gods and goddesses were related to each other. Study the chart on gods and goddesses, and use the information to fill out the family tree below. (Remember to write in both the Greek and Roman names for each god or goddess.)

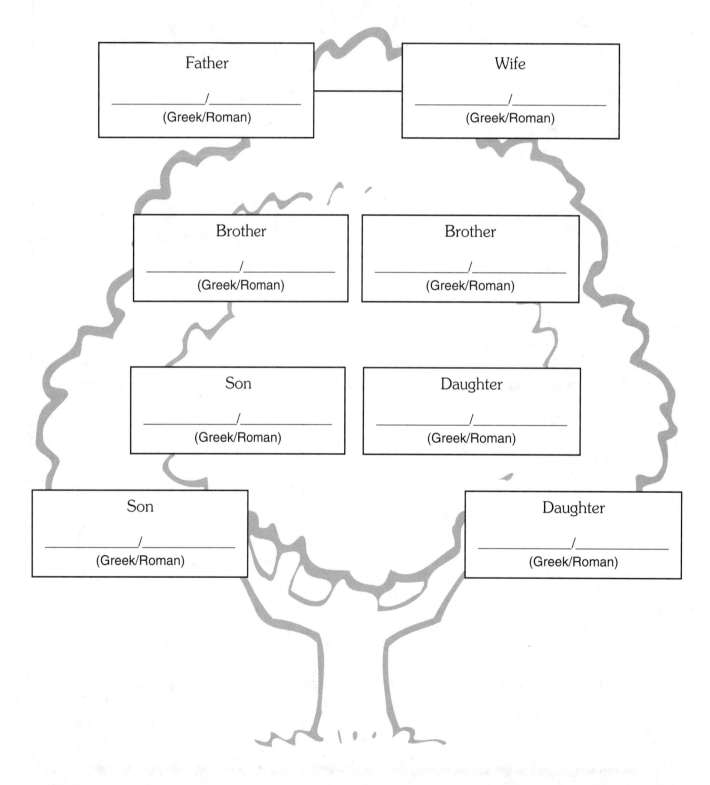

Father

_____ / _____
(Greek/Roman)

Wife

_____ / _____
(Greek/Roman)

Brother

_____ / _____
(Greek/Roman)

Brother

_____ / _____
(Greek/Roman)

Son

_____ / _____
(Greek/Roman)

Daughter

_____ / _____
(Greek/Roman)

Son

_____ / _____
(Greek/Roman)

Daughter

_____ / _____
(Greek/Roman)

Study the clues below. Then draw a circle around either Middle East or Africa to indicate where the action occurred.

1. Two types of writing are developed—cuneiform and hieroglyphics.

   Middle East   **Africa**

2. Kingdom of Kush becomes a major center of art, learning, and trade.

   Middle East   **Africa**

3. Iron is used to make tools and weapons.

   Middle East   **Africa**

4. Alexander the Great builds an empire from Egypt to India.

   Middle East   **Africa**

5. Moses leads the Hebrew people to Palestine.

   Middle East   **Africa**

6. The Kingdom of Axum becomes a prosperous trading center for ivory.

   Middle East   **Africa**

7. The wheel is invented.

   Middle East   **Africa**

8. The Islamic religion spreads from one continent to another.

   Middle East   **Africa**

9. Ghana controls the trade in gold.

   Middle East   **Africa**

10. The world's first cities are built.

    Middle East   **Africa**

Find the names of famous people and places from the ancient Middle East and Africa. You can use the name bank for help.

1. He founded the Christian religion.

   _____

2. These people were known for their terra-cotta sculptures of heads.

   _____

3. He built an empire from Egypt to India.

   _____

4. It is the first known African state south of the Sahara Desert.

   _____

5. They are buried in the Egyptian pyramids.

   _____

6. The world's first cities were built here.

   _____

7. It became a wealthy trading center for ivory.

   _____

8. He united the Hebrews into one strong kingdom.

   _____

Name Bank

King David   Alexander the Great

Mesopotamia   Ghana

Kingdom of Axum   pharaohs

Jesus Christ   Nok culture

Answer these questions about the ancient Middle East. You can use the word bank for help.

1. I was the king of Macedonia. I built a great empire.

   —— —— —— —— —— —— —— —— —— —— —— —— —— —— —— —— —— ——

2. We are buried in the pyramids in the Egyptian desert.

   —— —— —— —— —— —— —— ——

3. I was the first type of writing developed by the Sumerians.

   —— —— —— —— —— —— —— —— ——

4. I was the prophet who lead the Hebrew People to Palestine.

   —— —— —— —— ——

5. I was the collection of the first written laws in Babylonia.

   —— —— —— —— —— —— —— —— —— —— —— —— —— ——

6. I founded the Christian religion.

   —— —— —— —— —— —— —— —— —— —— ——

7. I was the first type of writing developed by the Egyptians.

   —— —— —— —— —— —— —— —— —— —— —— —— ——

8. In 1000 B.C., I united the Hebrews in one strong kingdom.

   —— —— —— —— —— —— —— —— ——

9. We conquered Palestine and made it part of our empire.

   —— —— —— —— —— ——

10. I was invaded by many different peoples after 1000 B.C.

    —— —— —— —— —— —— —— —— ——

Word Bank

Moses	Alexander the Great	cuneiform
King David	Palestine	Code of Hammurabi
Jesus Christ	Pharaohs	hieroglyphics
	Romans	

Use page 32 to help you find the answers referred to in each of these headlines. Use the word bank for help.

1. Nigerians Creates Headlines with Terra-Cotta Sculptures

   _____

2. Religion Spreads across North Africa, Enters Spain

   _____

3. State South of Sahara Controls Gold Trade

   _____

4. A.D. 350 Sees Kingdom's Death

   _____

5. Tools and Weapons Make Use of Underground Material

   _____

6. Ivory Hits Market in Arabian Kingdom

   _____

7. New Language Hits Eastern and Southern Africa from West

   _____

8. Little Known About Lives of Ancients

   _____

Word Bank

Bantu	Kush	Islam
Ghana	Sub-Saharan Africans	Axum
Nok culture	iron	

Unscramble the letters to form words. In the appropriate space on the chart, explain how this word is related to ancient African history. You can use the word bank for help. The first one has been done for you.

Scrambled Word	Real Word	How Is It Related?
1. godinKm fo shuK	Kingdom of Kush	major center of African art, learning, and trade
2. clmalis igoneril		
3. koN tuleruc		
4. haraaS rtseeD		
5. giNre reiRv		
6. potEihai		
7. steW rAcfia		
8. hanGa		
9. yirov		
10. neatdiMeraner ase		

Word Bank

ivory	Sahara Desert	Kingdom of Kush
Mediterranean Sea	Islamic religion	Ethiopia
West Africa	Niger River	Ghana
		Nok culture

Study the clues and the name bank below. Then write down the name of each famous person or group in ancient Asian history.

1. I made the Chinese language the same throughout the country.

_____

2. We overthrew the Shang peoples around 1050 B.C.

_____

3. My rules for how people should treat each other are still followed in China today.

_____

4. I united Northern India.

_____

5. We used a kind of writing based on pictures which developed into today's Chinese writing.

_____

6. I founded the Buddhist religion.

_____

7. We won control of all of China in 202 B.C.

_____

8. I sent Buddhist missionaries into southern Asia to spread Buddhism.

_____

9. We developed gunpowder and paper.

_____

10. It spread throughout India beginning around 1500 B.C.

_____

Name Bank

Ancient Chinese inventors	Chandragupta Maurya	Chou peoples
Confucius	Shang peoples	Asoka
Shih Huang Ti	Han peoples	Hindu religion
Ghana	Siddhartha Gautama	

Study the clues below. Then circle **Ancient Europe** or **The Americas** to show where the action occurred.

1. Native people lived in places called pueblos.

    Ancient Europe   **The Americas**

2. People hunted buffalo for clothing and food.

    Ancient Europe   **The Americas**

3. People built big palaces and megaliths.

    Ancient Europe   **The Americas**

4. Colonists moved in and later brought with them African-American slaves.

    Ancient Europe   **The Americas**

5. Socrates, Plato, and Aristotle were great philosophers.

    Ancient Europe   **The Americas**

6. People invented democratic government.

    Ancient Europe   **The Americas**

7. Warriors made human sacrifices.

    Ancient Europe   **The Americas**

8. The Spanish brought diseases which killed native peoples.

    Ancient Europe   **The Americas**

9. One of their wars became a part of poetry and mythology.

    Ancient Europe   **The Americas**

10. People from England sailed over to the land.

    Ancient Europe   **The Americas**

Fill in the crossword puzzle by answering the clues below.

Across

3. The battle between invading Greeks and the people of Troy was called the _____.

6. _____ the Great conquered lands from the Mediterranean Sea to India.

7. King Philip II of _____ conquered all the cities of Greece.

8. Between 2500 B.C. and 1200 B.C., Mycenaean people invaded _____.

Down

1. _____ in England is an example of a megalith.

2. The _____ on the Acropolis is an example of Greek architecture.

4. _____ won the Peloponnesian Wars.

5. The _____ is a poem about the travels of Odysseus.

Use this code to identify these anniversaries from 1903 and 1904. For example, A = 1.

A	B	C	D	E	F	G	H	I	J	K	L	M	N	O	P	Q	R	S	T	U	V	W	X	Y	Z
1	2	3	4	5	6	7	8	9	10	11	12	13	14	15	16	17	18	19	20	21	22	23	24	25	26

1. These were held in St. Louis, Missouri to celebrate the 100th anniversary of the Louisiana Purchase.

    ___ ___ ___ ___ ___ ___ ___   ___ ___ ___ ___ ___
    15 12 25 13 16   9   3   7   1 13   5 19

2. This silent film became the first major American movie with a realistic plot.

    ___ ___ ___ ___ ___   ___ ___ ___ ___ ___
     7 18   5   1 20   20 18   1   9 14

    ___ ___ ___ ___ ___ ___ ___
    18 15   2   2   5 18 25

3. He became the first player in major league history to pitch a perfect game.

    ___ ___ ___ ___ ___ ___   ___ ___ ___ ___
     4   5 14 20 15 14   20 18 21   5

    ___ ___ ___ ___ ___
    25 15 21 14   7

4. Bicycle riders raced 1,500 miles across France in this.

    ___ ___ ___ ___   ___ ___   ___ ___ ___ ___ ___ ___
    20 15 21 18   4   5   6 18   1 14   3   5

5. She led hundreds of workers in a march to protest long hours of factory and mill work.

    ___ ___ ___ ___   ___ ___ ___ ___ ___ ___
    13   1 18 25   8   1 18 18   9 19

    ___ ___ ___ ___ ___
    10 15 14   5 19

6. These were published as collections of cartoons that had already appeared in newspapers.

    ___ ___ ___ ___ ___   ___ ___ ___ ___ ___
     3 15 13   9   3   2 15 15 11 19

7. She was both blind and deaf, but still graduated from Radcliffe College.

    ___ ___ ___ ___ ___   ___ ___ ___ ___ ___ ___
     8   5 12   5 14   11   5 12 12   5 18

8. He made the first successful flight in Kitty Hawk, North Carolina.

    ___ ___ ___ ___ ___ ___ ___   ___ ___ ___ ___ ___ ___
    15 18 22   9 12 12   5   23 18   9   7   8 20

These imaginary Web sites would lead you to information about famous people or events in 1903 and 1904. Answer each one with a name. Use the name bank for help.

1. www.factorieshurt/kids

   _____

2. www.blindanddeaf/college.grad

   _____

3. www.ridemybike/France.tour

   _____

4. www.perfectgame/major.league

   _____

5. www.quietfilm.trains/robbery

   _____

6. www.nobelprize.radium/polonium

   _____

7. www.webeatyou.five/three

   _____

8. www.flyinghigh/Kittyhawk

   _____

Name Bank

Orville Wright	Boston Pilgrims
Tour de France	Mary Harris Jones
Denton True Young	The Great Train Robbery
Pierre and Marie Curie	Helen Keller

Here is a list of inventions in the field of transportation over the last few centuries.

Inventions Take Us From One Place To Another		
YEAR	**INVENTION**	**INVENTOR (COUNTRY)**
1785	parachute	Jean Pierre Blanchard (France)
1807	steamboat (practical)	Robert Fulton (U.S.)
1829	steam locomotive	George Stephenson (England)
1852	elevator	Elisha G. Otis (U.S.)
1885	bicycle	James Starley (England)
1885	motorcycle	Gottlieb Daimler (Germany)
1891	escalator	Jesse W. Reno (U.S.)
1892	automobile (gasoline)	Charles E. Duryea & J. Frank Duryea (U.S.)
1894	submarine	Simon Lake (U.S.)
1895	diesel engine	Rudolf Diesel (Germany)
1903	propeller airplane	Orville & Wilbur Wright (U.S.)
1939	helicopter	Igor Sikorsky (U.S.)
1939	jet airplane	Hans van Ohain (Germany)
1973	Jet Ski®	Clayton Jacobsen II (U.S)
1980	rollerblades	Scott Olson (U.S.)
2001	Segway Human Transport* *a computer-controlled electric scooter	Dean Kamen (U.S.) ©

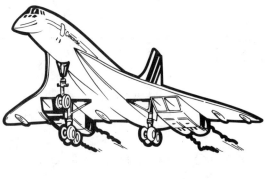

These inventions are responsible for saving countless lives.

Inventions Help Us Live Healthier and Longer Lives		
YEAR	**INVENTION**	**INVENTOR (COUNTRY)**
1780	bifocal lenses for glasses	Benjamin Franklin (U.S.)
1819	stethoscope	René T.M.H. Laënnec (France)
1842	anesthesia (ether)	Crawford W. Long (U.S.)
1895	X-ray	Wilhelm Roentgen (Germany)
1922	insulin	Sir Frederick G. Banting (Canada)
1923	automatic traffic signal	Garrett A. Morgan (U.S.)
1929	penicillin	Alexander Fleming (Scotland)
1952	airbag	John Hetrick (U.S.)
1954	antibiotic for fungal diseases	R. F. Brown & E. L. Hazen (U.S.)
1955	polio vaccine	Jonas E. Salk (U.S.)
1973	CAT scanner	Godfrey N. Hounsfield (England)
1978	artificial heart	Robert K. Jarvik (U.S.)
1987	meningitis vaccine	Connaught Lab (U.S.)
2000	self-contained artificial heart	Robert K. Jarvik (U.S.)

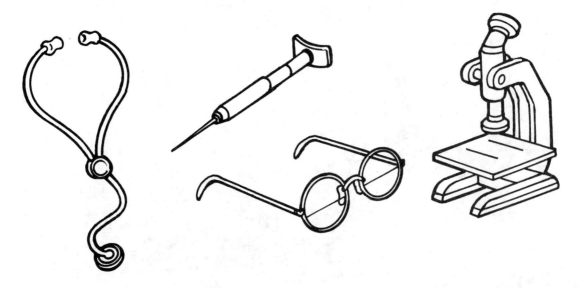

Chances are, you've used at least one of the following inventions within the last day or so.

Inventions Help Us Communicate With One Another

YEAR	INVENTION	INVENTOR (COUNTRY)
105	paper	Ts'ai Lun (China)
1447	movable type	Johann Gutenberg (Germany)
1795	modern pencil	Nicolas Jacques Conté (France)
1837	telegraph	Samuel F.B. Morse (U.S.)
1845	rotary printing press	Richard M. Hoe (U.S.)
1867	typewriter	Christopher L. Sholes, Carlos Glidden, & Samuel W. Soulé (U.S.)
1870s	telephone	Alexander G. Bell (U.S.); Antonio Meucci (Italy)
1888	ballpoint pen	John Loud (U.S.)
1913	modern radio receiver	Reginald A. Fessenden (U.S.)
1937	xerography copies	Chester Carlson (U.S.)
1942	electronic computer	John V. Atanasoff & Clifford Berry (U.S.)
1944	auto sequence computer	Howard H. Aiken (U.S.)
1947	transistor	William Shockley, Walter H. Brattain, & John Bardeen (U.S.)
1955	fiber optics	Narinder S. Kapany (England)
1965	word processor	IBM (U.S.)
1979	cellular telephone	Ericsson Company (Sweden)
1987	laptop computer	Sir Clive Sinclair (England) ©
1994	digital camera	Apple Computer, Kodak (U.S.)
2002	wind-up cell phone	Motorola (U.S.) & Freeplay Energy Group (England)

What did people used to do for fun? Without the following inventions, you wouldn't have as many entertainment options as you do today.

Inventions Entertain Us		
YEAR	**INVENTION**	**INVENTOR (COUNTRY)**
1709	piano	Bartolomeo Cristofori (Italy)
1877	phonograph	Thomas A. Edison (U.S.)
1877	microphone	Emile Berliner (U.S.)
1888	portable camera	George Eastman (U.S.)
1893	moving picture viewer	Thomas A. Edison (U.S.)
1894	motion picture projector	Charles F. Jenkins (U.S.)
1899	tape recorder	Valdemar Poulsen (Denmark)
1923	television*	Vladimir K. Zworykin* (U.S.)
1963	audiocassette	Phillips Corporation (Netherlands)
1963	steel tennis racquet	René Lacoste (France)
1969	videotape cassette	Sony (Japan)
1972	compact disc (CD)	RCA (U.S.)
1972	video game (Pong)	Noland Bushnell (U.S.)
1979	Walkman	Sony (Japan)
1995	DVD (digital video disk)	Matsushita (Japan)

Others who helped invent television include Philo T. Farnsworth (1926) and John Baird (1928).

Some inventions save lives. Some give us exciting new ways to experience life. But others just make our day-to-day lives a little easier. Those inventions are important, too!

Inventions Make Our Lives Easier

YEAR	INVENTION	INVENTOR (COUNTRY)
1752	lightning rod	Benjamin Franklin (U.S.)
1800	electric battery	Alessandro Volta (Italy)
1831	lawn mower	Edwin Budding & John Ferrabee (England)
1834	refrigeration	Jacob Perkins (England)
1846	sewing machine	Elias Howe (U.S.)
1851	cylinder (door) lock	Linus Yale (U.S.)
1079	practical light bulb	Thomas A. Edison (U.S.)
1886	dishwasher	Josephine Cochran (U.S.)
1891	zipper	Whitcomb L. Judson (U.S.)
1901	washing machine	Langmuir Fisher (U.S.)
1903	windshield wipers	Mary Anderson (U.S.)
1907	vacuum cleaner	J. Murray Spangler (U.S.)
1911	air conditioning	Willis H. Carrier (U.S.)
1924	frozen packaged food	Clarence Birdseye (U.S.)
1948	Velcro	Georges de Mestral (Switzerland)
1958	laser	A. L. Schawlow & C. H. Townes (U.S.)
1963	pop-top can	Ermal C. Fraze (U.S.)
1969	cash machine (ATM)	Don Wetzel (U.S.)
1971	food processor	Pierre Verdon (France)
1980	Post-its	3M Company (U.S.)
1981	Polartec fabric	Malden Mills (U.S.)
2001	MET5 heat-generating jacket	Malden Ventures, Polartec, & North Face (U.S.)

The following inventions have furthered our quest to know more about our world—from its smallest, microscopic details to the huge expanses of space.

Inventions Help Us Expand Our Universe

YEAR	INVENTION	INVENTOR (COUNTRY)
1250	magnifying glass	Roger Bacon (England)
1590	2-lens microscope	Zacharias Janssen (Netherlands)
1608	telescope	Hans Lippershey (Netherlands)
1714	mercury thermometer	Gabriel D. Fahrenheit (Germany)
1926	rocket engine	Robert H. Goddard (U.S.)
1930	cyclotron (atom smasher)	Ernest O. Lawrence (U.S.)
1943	Aqua Lung	Jacques-Yves Cousteau & Emile Gagnan (France)
1977	space shuttle	NASA (U.S.)
2001	EZ-Rocket (reusable rocket engines)	Jeff Greason (U.S.)

To learn more about inventions and the people who created them, or to make your own invention, visit

Inventure Place
National Inventors Hall of Fame
221 S. Broadway, Akron, Ohio 44308
Phone: (330) 762-4463.
E-mail: museum@invent.org
WEB SITE *http://www.invent.org*

Match the inventor to the invention.

_____ 1. anesthesia

_____ 2. meningitis vaccine

_____ 3. airbag

_____ 4. lightning rod

_____ 5. polio vaccine

_____ 6. X-ray

_____ 7. stethoscope

_____ 8. insulin

_____ 9. self-contained artificial heart

_____ 10. CAT scanner

a. Connaught Lab

b. Wilhelm Roentgen

c. René T.M.H. Laënnec

d. John Hetrick

e. Robert K. Jarvik

f. Jonas E. Salk

g. Sir Frederick G. Banting

h. Godfrey N. Hounsfield

i. Crawford W. Long

j. Benjamin Franklin

For over 300 years, people have been inventing things to help us live healthier and longer lives. Use these clues to identify some of these inventions.

1. We've been injecting people with this since 1955 to keep them from getting sick.

   P ___ ___ ___ O   V ___ ___ ___ ___ N ___

2. In 1978, this invention meant that people with bad hearts could go on living.

   A ___ ___ ___ F ___ ___ ___ ___ L   ___ E ___ ___ T

3. This invention allows you to have surgery without ever feeling a thing.

   A ___ ___ ___ ___ H ___ ___ I A

4. These allow people to read both close up and far away.

   B ___ ___ ___ C ___ ___   L ___ ___ S ___ ___

5. This lets the doctor listen to your heartbeat.

   ___ T ___ ___ H ___ ___ C ___ ___ ___ ___

6. This invention allows doctors to look inside your brain.

   ___ ___ T   S ___ ___ ___ N ___ R

7. This invention helps people with diabetes to live longer, happier lives.

   I ___ ___ ___ L ___ ___

8. This lets doctors take a look inside your body.

   ___ - ___ ___ Y

Decide which invention would work best for you in the following situations. You can use the word bank below for help.

1. You fell off your bike and broke your arm.

_____

2. You need to have surgery to remove your tonsils.

_____

3. You have trouble seeing things up close, but your long-distance vision is fine.

_____

4. There's a fire in your house.

_____

5. You're driving in your car when you swerve to avoid a dog, and your car hits a tree.

_____

6. You forget about the rice cooking on the stove, and it burns.

_____

7. You fall while skiing and knock yourself unconscious.

_____

8. You have an ear infection.

_____

9. You discover you have a bad case of athlete's foot.

_____

10. There's a thunder and lightning storm outside your house.

_____

Word Bank

lightning rod	bifocal lenses for glasses	X-ray
penicillin	CAT scan	fire extinguisher
anesthesia	antibiotic for fungal diseases	airbag
smoke detector		

Study the inventions that take us from one place to another, then answer the questions below. Use the word bank for help.

1. Which invention would you be glad to have if your propeller airplane broke down?

   _____

2. What could get you across the country the fastest if your helicopter wasn't working?

   _____

3. What would be most helpful in getting you to the 32nd floor of a skyscraper?

   _____

4. Which would give you more exercise—rollerblades or the Segway Human Transport?

   _____

5. Which invention was necessary before the diesel engine could be invented?

   _____

6. Which invention is propelled by steam?

   _____

7. Which came first—the automobile or the motorcycle?

   _____

8. What would you use if you had to get from one side of a lake to another in a hurry?

   _____

9. Which invention allows you to travel under water?

   _____

10. Which inventions allow you to travel both up and down?

   _____

Word Bank

steam engine	submarine	jet airplane
dirigible	parachute	escalator
Jet Ski	elevator	motorcycle
escalator	rollerblades	helicopter

Analogy puzzles are thinking games involving relationships between paired items. Finding the relationship between the given pair of the analogy will give you the key to solving the second part. Use the page on transportation inventions to solve these analogies.

1. Robert Fulton is to the steamboat as ___Gottlieb Daimler___ is to the motorcycle.

2. France is to Jean Pierre Blanchard as _____ is to Dean Kamen.

3. 1903 is to the propeller airplane as 1829 is to the _____ .

4. Elisha J. Otis is to the elevator as Igor Sikorsky is to the

_____ .

5. Germany is to Gottlieb Daimler as _____ is to

Clayton Jacobsen.

6. George Stephenson is to the steam locomotive as _____ is to rollerblades.

7. The submarine is to Simon Lake as the _____ is to Orville and Wilbur Wright.

9. James Starley is to England as Hans van Ohain is to _____ .

10. Rudolf Diesel is to the diesel engine as _____ is to the escalator.

A car license plate can tell something about its owner. Decode these plates to reveal clues to the names of inventors or companies who help us communicate with one another. You can use the name bank for help. In the word bank, each person or company's invention is listed in parentheses.

1.

_____

2.

_____

3.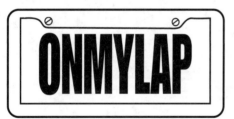

_____

4.

_____

5.

_____

6.

_____

7.

_____

8.

_____

Name Bank

Sir Clive Sinclair _(laptop computer)_

John Loud _(ballpoint pen)_

Ts'ai Lun _(paper)_

Alexander G. Bell _(telephone)_

Nicolas Jacques Conte _(modern pencil)_

Apple Computer, Kodak _(digital camera)_

Chester Carlson _(xerographic copies)_

Samuel F.B. Morse _(telegraph)_

Study the inventions below, and check the box after the invention that came first.

1. microscope ☐   *or*   telescope ☐

2. DVD ☐   *or*   piano ☐

3. X-Ray ☐   *or*   CAT scanner ☐

4. propeller airplane ☐   *or*   jet airplane ☐

5. windshield wipers ☐   *or*   automobile ☐

6. typewriter ☐   *or*   computer ☐

7. artificial heart ☐   *or*   stethoscope ☐

8. DVD ☐   *or*   audiocassette ☐

9. space shuttle ☐   *or*   rocket engine ☐

10. television ☐   *or*   video game ☐

Answer each clue with a word that contains double letters. Use the word bank below for help.

1. Benjamin Franklin invented bifocal lenses for these.

_____

2. Orville and Wilbur Wright invented this type of airplane.

_____

3. He invented the modern radio receiver.

_____

4. Alexander Fleming from Scotland invented this medicine.

_____

5. A United States company called I.B.M. invented this machine.

_____

6. He invented the stethoscope.

_____

7. John Loud invented this type of pen.

_____

8. Scott Olsen invented these to get around town.

_____

9. The meningitis vaccine was invented here.

_____

10. The Ericsson Company invented this type of telephone.

_____

Word Bank

Reginald A. Fessenden	René T.M.H. Laënnec	Connaught Lab
propeller	cellular	rollerblades
eyeglasses	word processor	penicillin
	ballpoint	

Answer the questions below. Use the word bank for help.

1. What would you use if you got a flat tire on the side of a road in the middle of the night?

   _____

2. What would you use if you wanted to surf the Internet on an airplane?

   _____

3. What would you use if you were writing an essay for a college class and the electricity went out at your house?

   _____

4. What would you use if you needed to write down your phone number for a friend?

   _____

5. What would you use if you wished to send photographs over the Internet to your family?

   _____

6. What would you use if you wanted to talk to your grandmother but she lives very far away?

   _____

7. What would you use if you wanted to write several drafts of a short story?

   _____

8. What would you use if you needed to hear a weather update and the electricity was out at your house?

   _____

Word Bank

cellular phone	digital camera
laptop computer	telephone
typewriter	computer
paper	transistor radio

These imaginary Web sites would lead you to information about the inventors who created items to entertain us. Answer each one with an inventor's name. Use the word bank for help.

1. www.discmusic/1972

_____

2. www.motionpix.viewme

_____

3. www.record/spinnplay

_____

4. www.tapeit/movies.VCR

_____

5. www.walkandsing/1979

_____

6. www.projectfilms/motion

_____

7. www.blackandwhite.keys

_____

8. www.hittheball/steel.strings

_____

9. www.shootandmove.film

_____

10. www.playtowin.tv/game

_____

Word Bank

Walkman	compact disc	videotape cassette
moving picture viewer	piano	video game
portable camera	phonograph	motion picture projector
	steel tennis racket	

Solve these mysteries with names of famous inventors or companies. Study the clues and the years given, then fill in the blanks.

1. **(1714)** He gave his name to part of this thermometer.

   ⇒ Who done it? _____

2. **(1752, 1780)** He came up with not one, but two inventions!

   ⇒ Who done it? _____

3. **(1980)** He changed the wheels on roller skates for a whole new way of skating!

   ⇒ Who done it? _____

4. **(1987)** He allowed us to take our computers wherever we want.

   ⇒ Who done it? _____

5. **(1924)** He put his name on every chilly package his invention came in.

   ⇒ Who done it? _____

6. **(1852)** He helped people in wheelchairs to get to the top floor.

   ⇒ Who done it? _____

7. **(1926)** His invention helped send people to the moon.

   ⇒ Who done it? _____

8. **(1979)** This company allowed us to run on the beach while listening to music.

   ⇒ Who done it? _____

Decode the picture to reveal the names of inventions that make our lives easier. Refer to pages 51–55 for help. Note: the words may be spelled phonetically.

1.

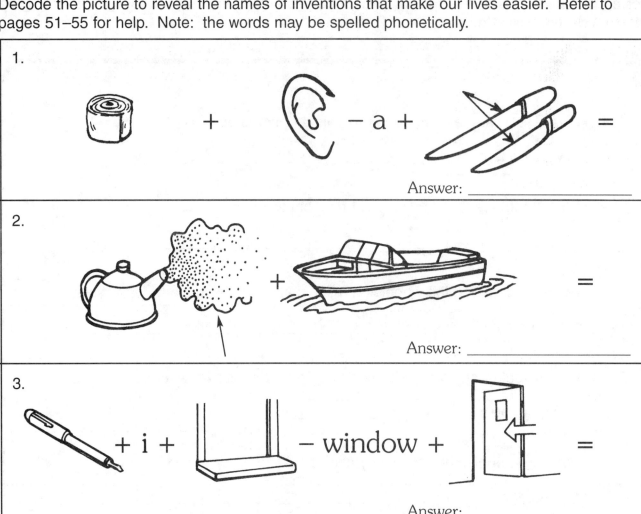

$+$ $-$ a $+$ $=$

Answer: _____

2.

$+$ $=$

Answer: _____

3.

$+$ i $+$ $-$ window $+$ $=$

Answer: _____

4.

$+$ **P** $+$ $=$

Answer: _____

5.

$+$ S $+$ C $+$ $-$ M $=$

Answer: _____

Read these clues about important inventions. Write the invention and the inventor's name in each blank to complete the chart. Use the word bank for help.

Description	Invention	Inventor's Name
1. This invention lets people cook a complete dinner in just ten minutes instead of an hour.		
2. This invention lets people fasten their tennis shoes in just seconds.		
3. This invention helps you drive safely through the rain.		
4. This invention lets you get money out of your account in almost any part of the world.		
5. This invention lets you enjoy leftover Chinese food for days after the original meal.		
6. This invention means your Halloween costume can be ready in one day instead of a week.		
7. This invention gets rid of dog hair quickly when you have unexpected guests.		
8. This invention lets you listen to the radio at the beach.		
9. This invention keeps you from forgetting important dates.		
10. This invention keeps you cool in the middle of summer.		

Word Bank

air conditioner	sewing machine	electric battery
Velcro	vacuum cleaner	refrigeration
cash machine	frozen packaged food	Post-it notes
	windshield wipers	

Decide which invention would work best for you in the following situations. Use the inventions bank for help.

1. You work in a gymnasium, where there are hundreds of dirty towels at the end of the day.

   _____

2. You need to check on your crying baby at three in the morning.

   _____

3. You want to chop up an onion without getting your hands dirty.

   _____

4. You're camping, and you want to close your sleeping bag.

   _____

5. You're writing a top-secret entry in your diary and you don't want to be bothered.

   _____

6. You brought a soda to the picnic, but not a can opener.

   _____

7. You find yourself lost in a snowstorm.

   _____

8. You've got to get the backyard looking nice for a party.

   _____

9. You've got five minutes to clean up the kitchen.

   _____

10. You see a dress your mother would love, but you forgot your checkbook.

    _____

Inventions Bank

electric light bulb	washing machine	lawn mower
Polartec fabric	zipper	food processor
cash machine	cylinder door lock	dishwasher
	pop-top can	

Fill in the blanks below and locate each underlined word in the Word Search. Words may go up, down, or horizontally. Use the word bank for help.

1. The _____ was invented by NASA in 1977.

2. Hans Lippershey invented the _____ in the Netherlands.

3. The _____ was invented in 1250 by Roger Bacon.

4. Jacques-Yves Costeau and Emile Gagnan invented the _____ in France.

5. In 1714, Gabriel D. Fahrenheit used his name as part of the _____.

6. Robert H. Goddard of the United States invented the _____.

7. In 2001, the _____ was invented in the United States.

8. The _____ by Ernest O. Lawrence is also called an atom smasher.

```
e x m g d o p w d i e m d l i s b m g i g o g s p
w e g a f e z r o c k e t b o i d s p s i p d m c
w g m i g g w o e n g s i o d m z e d l s m c i o
w e g k d n w m d i g m e i o w t e g s k i c l s
c w d g i e i w e d g j r o c k e t e n g i n e h
y s d w e i s f w e m d i g l e l s p e o d e i m
c g m e r c u r y t h e r m o m e t e r p r w e t
l s d i g m e k w i w d i o g m s s g i o e m s r
o d m d i a w e m g n w e m i g c w e g m i d t q
t s m i t q w e m i t g e m i d o w d m k c b l d
r w d m i u e m s i o t g w e m p w e d p o d m g
o e m s p a c e s h u t t l e x e s p o e d m r t
n w e m i l e m i d g e w p a x p l m c b n k d d
s m e i o u w e m i d g o w d s p x l d m r n g d
a s m i d n e s i o j g e k d e s p o e m i b m f
s t m i d g x c n m b d p w m i o p d k g m k e r
```

Word Bank

mercury thermometer	Aqua Lung	EZ-Rocket
telescope	space shuttle	rocket engine
cyclotron	magnifying glass	

Match the invention to the situation for which it would be best used.

_____ 1. telescope

_____ 2. portable camera

_____ 3. laptop computer

_____ 4. X-ray

_____ 5. refrigerator

_____ 6. elevator

_____ 7. vacuum cleaner

_____ 8. tape recorder

_____ 9. space shuttle

_____ 10. automobile

a. Your little brother may have swallowed a quarter.

b. You need to get from the 30th floor to the ground floor of a building in a hurry.

c. You want to hear how you sound when you sing The Star-Spangled Banner.

d. You're going to the Grand Canyon and want to have something by which to remember your trip.

e. You want your soccer team to enjoy cold drinks after practice in your backyard.

f. You want to take a trip across the country and stop wherever you want, whenever you want.

g. The dog found a box of cookies, and there are crumbs all over the carpet.

h. You have an important paper due for school, but you have to fly across the country to see your grandparents.

i. You want to know whether life exists on Mars.

j. Meteorologists report that Saturn is passing close to the earth and can be viewed at midnight.

Transportation

What would people from the 1600s, or the 1800s, think if they could come back and look at the world today? They would get lots of surprises. One surprise would be how fast people can travel to distant places.

HOW LONG DID IT TAKE?

1620 — The *Mayflower* took 66 days to sail across the Atlantic from Plymouth, England, to present-day Provincetown, Massachusetts.

1819 — The first Atlantic Ocean crossing by a ship powered in part by steam (*Savannah*, from Savannah, Georgia, to Liverpool, England) took 27 days.

1845 — A trip from Missouri to California by "wagon train" (covered wagons, usually pulled by oxen) took 4-5 months.

1854 — The clipper ship *Flying Cloud* sailed from New York to San Francisco (going around the tip of South America) in a record 89 days, 8 hours.

1876 — The *Transcontinental Express*, celebrating the U.S. centennial, crossed the country by rail from New York to San Francisco, in a record 83 hours, 39 minutes.

1927 — Charles Lindbergh flew from New York to Paris in 33½ hours. It was the first nonstop flight made across the Atlantic by one person.

1952 — The passenger ship *United States* set a record when it crossed the Atlantic in 3 days, 10 hours, and 40 minutes.

1969 — *Apollo 11*, averaging 3,417 mph, took just under four days to reach the moon (about 70 times the distance from London to New York).

1981 — At a speed of about 17,500 miles per hour, space shuttle *Columbia* circled the globe in 90 minutes.

1990 — A U.S. Air Force SR-71 "Blackbird" flew coast-to-coast in 1 hour, 7 minutes, and 54 seconds (at an average speed of 2,124 miles per hour).

1995 — Two Air Force B-1B bombers flew around the world nonstop (refueling in flight) in 36 hours and 13 minutes.

1996 — A British Airways Concorde jet flew from New York to London in 2 hours, 53 minutes.

1999 — Bertrand Piccard and Brian Jones completed the first around-the-world balloon flight in the *Breitling Orbiter 3*. It took 19 days, 21 hours, 55 minutes.

2002 — Steve Fossett sailed across the Atlantic from New York to Cornwall, England. It took 4 days, 17 hours, 28 minutes.

The first successful steam locomotive was built in England in 1804. Richard Trevithick's engine pulled 24,000 pounds of iron, 70 men, and 5 wagons along a 9.5-mile track. In 1830 the Baltimore and Ohio introduced America's first steam locomotive, the "Tom Thumb," to haul both passengers and freight. America's first transcontinental railroad was built from 1862 to 1869. Other railroad lines followed quickly over the next decades. In 1893, the first electrified rail line went into service, in Baltimore. Diesel engines were introduced in 1928, and streamlined trains began to appear in 1934.

The most famous modern high-speed train is the Shinkansen (Bullet Train), introduced in Japan in 1964. It can go as fast as 130 miles per hour. In 1981 France launched the Train à Grande Vitesse (TGV), which runs commercially at speeds of up to 186 mph. In the U.S. in 2000, Amtrak introduced Acela Express 150-mph high-speed service between Boston and Washington, D.C. Japan Railway is testing Maglev (MAGnetic LEVitation) trains. These use huge magnetic forces to lift trains above the track and send them forward on electical currents. The lack of friction helps them cruise at speeds of around 280 mph, and they have reached a record speed of 343 mph.

74

In 1886 Gottlieb Daimler patented a three-wheeled motor carriage in Germany. That same year, Karl Benz produced his first successful gasoline-powered vehicle. John W. Lambert of Ohio made the first gas-powered automobile in the U.S. in 1891.

Five years later, the Duryea Brothers of Springfield, Massachusetts, started the first car manufacturing company in the U.S. Henry Ford came soon after. In 1913 his use of an assembly line to produce the Model T revolutionized the automobile industry, making cars affordable for large numbers of people. Many improvements were made over the years, such as the first aerodynamically designed car, the Chrysler Airflow (1934), and air-conditioning, introduced by the Packard company in 1940. Ferdinand Porsche's Volkswagen "beetle," mass-produced after World War II, was one of the most popular cars in history.

Today's cars have computer-run features that make them safer and more efficient. Some even have the Global Positioning System to help you get where you want to go. But the main focus for developing the car of the future is fuel efficiency. Scientists all over the world are working on designing alternative-fuel cars. Zero Emission Vehicles (ZEVs) that use hydrogen cells to make electricity are one promising possibility.

EARLY AIRCRAFT

In 1783, the Montgolfier brothers flew the first hot air balloon over Paris. Another Frenchman, Henri Giffard, flew the first dirigible (blimp) in 1852. It was powered by steam. The first heavier-than-air flying machine was also steam-powered. Samuel P. Langley of the Smithsonian Institution in Washington, D.C., built a model plane with a 12-foot wingspan that flew nearly a mile in 1896. Wilbur and Orville Wright had been experimenting with heavier-than-air machines at the same time. In 1903 they traveled from their bicycle shop in Dayton, Ohio, to Kitty Hawk, North Carolina. Here they made four successful manned flights on December 17, launching the air age.

MILESTONES IN AVIATION

Airlines were first developed in the U.S. to carry mail. Transcontinental service was launched in 1921, bringing mail from San Francisco to New York in 33 hours—3 times faster than by train. By 1926, regular airmail service was in place, and a pilot named Charles A. Lindbergh was flying the Chicago-to-St. Louis route. Passenger service was well under way by 1930.

Aircraft continued to get bigger and faster. In 1936, the DC-3 set a record flying from Los Angeles to Newark, New Jersey, in 13 hours and 4 minutes. In 1959 the Boeing 707 was launched. It was the first successful passenger jet. The Boeing 707 could carry 180 passengers at 550 miles per hour—about 225 mph faster than propeller-powered airliners. One of the most famous airliners to be developed was the Boeing 747 "jumbo jet," introduced in 1969. Cruising at 566 mph, it can carry about 500 passengers. By around 2005, Boeing hopes to introduce the Sonic Cruiser. This radically designed jet would carry 225 passengers up to 11,500 miles nonstop at speeds of 725 mph.

Ships are used for many activities, from fishing, to vacationing, to exploration, to war. But their most important job has always been carrying cargo. The Egyptians were building reed and wooden sailboats some 5,000 years ago. They also built wooden barges over 200 feet long that could carry close to 2,000,000 pounds of cargo.

By the 1500s, huge sailing ships called galleons were hauling cargo around the world. Spanish galleons carried gold, spices, and other riches back to Europe from South America. These ships had to be big and needed cannons to defend themselves from pirates. Later cargo ships did without cannons. Packet ships began regularly scheduled passenger service across the Atlantic in 1818. In the 1840s, the U.S. built the first clipper ships. With a slender hull and many sails, they were the fastest ships of the pre-steam era.

The world's biggest ship today is the supertanker *Jahre Viking*. It's 1,502 feet long. That's longer than the Empire State building is tall. The *Jahre Viking* can carry 4.2 million barrels of oil. The *Queen Mary 2*, scheduled to be finished in 2003, will be the largest passenger ship ever. It will be 23 stories high and 1,131 feet long. That's almost 150 feet longer than the height of Eiffel Tower.

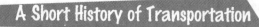

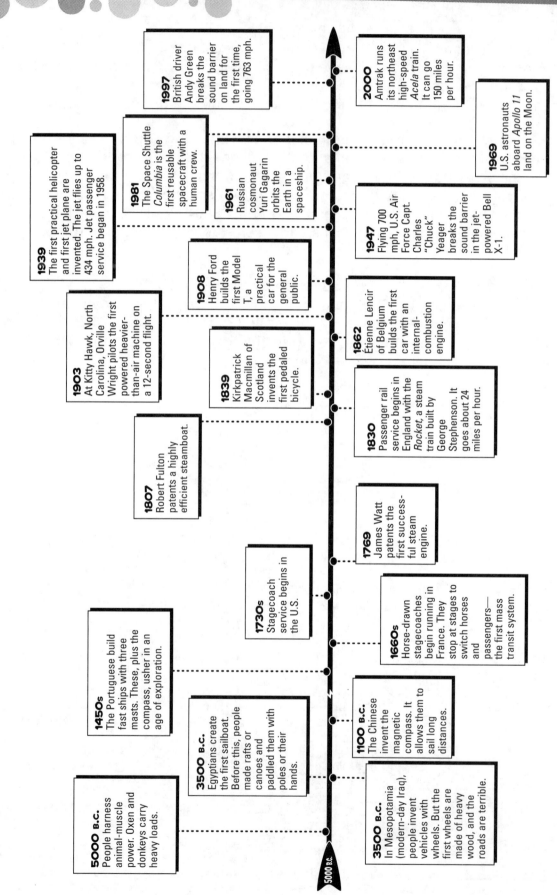

1997 British driver Andy Green breaks the sound barrier on land for the first time, going 763 mph.

2000 Amtrak runs its northeast high-speed *Acela* train. It can go 150 miles per hour.

1969 U.S. astronauts aboard *Apollo 11* land on the Moon.

1939 The first practical helicopter and first jet plane are invented. The jet flies up to 434 mph. Jet passenger service began in 1958.

1981 The Space Shuttle *Columbia* is the first reusable spacecraft with a human crew.

1961 Russian cosmonaut Yuri Gagarin orbits the Earth in a spaceship.

1947 Flying 700 mph, U.S. Air Force Capt. Charles "Chuck" Yeager breaks the sound barrier in the jet-powered Bell X-1.

1903 At Kitty Hawk, North Carolina, Orville Wright pilots the first powered heavier-than-air machine on a 12-second flight.

1908 Henry Ford builds the first Model T, a practical car for the general public.

1862 Étienne Lenoir of Belgium builds the first car with an internal-combustion engine.

1839 Kirkpatrick Macmillan of Scotland invents the first pedaled bicycle.

1807 Robert Fulton patents a highly efficient steamboat.

1830 Passenger rail service begins in England with the *Rocket*, a steam train built by George Stephenson. It goes about 24 miles per hour.

1769 James Watt patents the first successful steam engine.

1730s Stagecoach service begins in the U.S.

1660s Horse-drawn stagecoaches begin running in France. They stop at stages to switch horses and passengers—the first mass transit system.

1450s The Portuguese build fast ships with three masts. These, plus the compass, usher in an age of exploration.

1100 B.C. The Chinese invent the magnetic compass. It allows them to sail long distances.

5000 B.C. People harness animal-muscle power. Oxen and donkeys carry heavy loads.

3500 B.C. Egyptians create the first sailboat. Before this, people made rafts or canoes and paddled them with poles or their hands.

3500 B.C. In Mesopotamia (modern-day Iraq), people invent vehicles with wheels. But the first wheels are made of heavy wood, and the roads are terrible.

5000 B.C.

Between 1620 and 2002, the speed of transportation increased greatly. Use the letters in the words "Go With the Flow" to answer the clues below.

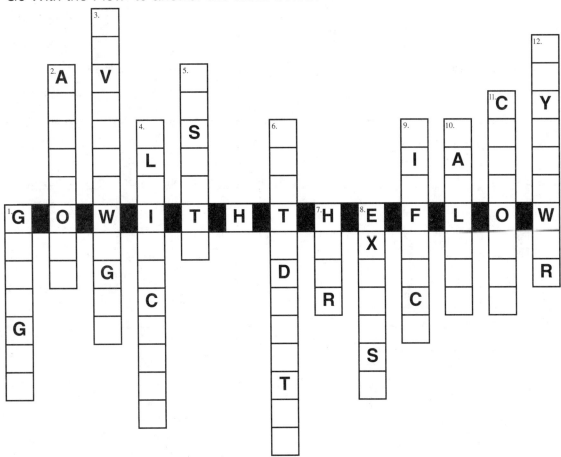

1. The steamboat *Savannah* left this state to arrive in England 27 days later.

2. It took just four days to reach the moon in 1969.

3. Often pulled by oxen, this took 4-5 months to travel from Missouri to California.

4. This clipper ship sailed from New York to San Francisco in a record 89 days, 8 hours.

5. It took him 4 days, 17, hours, and 38 minutes to sail across the Atlantic in 2002.

6. In 1952, this passenger ship set a record, crossing the Atlantic in 3 days, 10 hours, and 40 minutes.

7. The space shuttle *Columbia* circled the globe at 17,500 miles per _____.

8. In 1876, this transcontinental train crossed the country in a record-breaking 83 hours and 39 minutes.

9. This branch of the armed forces created two B-1B bombers that flew around the world nonstop in 36 hours and 13 minutes.

10. Bertrand Piccard and Brian Jones spent 19 days, 21 hours, and 55 minutes traveling around the world in this.

11. This British Airways jet flew from New York to London in 2 hours and 53 minutes in 1996.

12. This spent 66 days on the sea from England to Massachusetts in 1620.

Write an appropriate question for each of the following answers. Use the question box below for help in beginning each question. The first one has been done for you.

Question Box

- Who?
- What?
- Where?
- When?
- Why?
- How?

---

1. British Airways Concorde Jet

   Question: <u>What was the name of the jet that flew from New York to London in 1996?</u>

2. Steve Fossett

   Question: _____

3. 1969

   Question: _____

4. Charles Lindbergh

   Question: _____

5. *The Mayflower*

   Question: _____

6. oxen

   Question: _____

7. 17,500 miles per hour

   Question: _____

8. Breitling Orbiter 3

   Question: _____

9. U.S. Air Force SR-71 "Blackbird"

   Question: _____

10. *Transcontinental Express*

    Question: _____

Unscramble the letters to fill in the blanks. Use the word bank below for help.

1. Built in 1804, this was the first successful _____
   (*meats cooltimove*).

2. The _____ (*hnksiasnen*) is the most famous modern high-speed train.

3. Japan Railway is testing trains that use _____ (*tagmenic scerof*)
   that lift trains above the track.

4. In 1893, the first _____ (*feeltedciri lari nile*)
   went into service in Baltimore.

5. Both passengers and freight could ride the _____ (*mot mbuth*) in 1830.

6. In 2000, Amtrak introduced a high-speed service between Washington D.C. and Boston
   called the _____ (*leaca xsepers*).

7. In 1928, _____ (*seedli seengin*) were introduced to the world of trains.

8. America's first _____ (*toncastrenlantin doirraal*)
   was built between 1862 and 1969.

9. Another name for the Japanese *Shinkansen* is the _____ (*tellub arint*).

10. France's _____ (*ratni a dearng eetsivs*)
    runs at speeds of up to 186 miles per hour.

Word Bank

Shinkansen	steam locomotive	transcontinental railroad
Train a Grande Vitesse	magnetic forces	Acela Express
Tom Thumb	bullet train	electrified rail line
	diesel engines	

Fill in the blanks to create a time line charting the automobile's progress.

1.

1886

Gottlieb Daimler

invented the

_____

_____

(invention)

3.

1891

_____

(inventor)

made the first
gas-powered
automobile in the
U.S.

5.

_____
(year)

Henry Ford

invented assembly
line production

6. **Post-WW II**

_____

(inventor)

mass-produced
the Volkswagen
"beetle"

2.

1886

_____

(inventor)

invented the
gasoline-powered
vehicle

4.

1896

Duryea Brothers

started the first

_____

_____

(business)

7.

2003–2004

the world's
scientists are
designing

_____

_____

(invention)

Using the clues, fill in the missing letters to spell words important to automobile history.

1. He produced the Model T using an assembly line.

   ____ e ____ ____ y   ____ o ____ d

2. The Zero Emission Vehicle uses these to make electricity.

   ____ y ____ ____ o g ____ ____   ____ e ____ ____ s

3. This continues to be one of the most popular cars in history.

   V ____ ____ k ____ ____ a ____ e ____   " ____ e ____ ____ l ____ "

4. The Chrysler Airflow was the first of these types of cars.

   ___ e r ___ ___ ___ n ___ m ___ ___ a ___ l ___   d ___ ___ i ___ n ___ d

5. This feature gets you where you want to go in today's cars.

   ___ l ___ ___ ___ l   P ___ ___ i ___ ___ ___ n ___ n ___   ___ y ___ ___ e ___

6. The three-wheeled motor carriage was built in this country.

   ____ ____ r ____ a ____ ____

7. The Duryea Brothers started the first American car-manufacturing company in this state.

   ____ a ____ ____ ____ c ____ ____ s ____ ____ t ____

8. Henry Ford's assembly line made cars this.

   a ____ ____ o ____ ____ a ____ l ____

9. This is the main focus for developing the car of the future.

   ____ u ____ ____   e ____ ____ i ____ ____ e ____ cy

10. Cars that used to run on gas may someday run on this.

    ___ l ___ ___ t ___ i ___ ___ t ___

A car license plate can tell something about its owner. Decode these plates to reveal clues to the names of famous people in the automobile industry. Use the name bank for help.

Name Bank

Karl Benz	Gottlieb Daimler	Henry Ford
Ferdinand Porsche	John W. Lambert	Duryea Brothers

1.

_____

2.

_____

3.

_____

4.

_____

5.

_____

6.

_____

7. **Now, design a license plate that gives clues about you!**

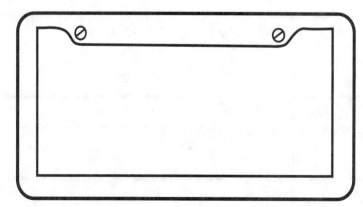

Use this code to identify these accomplishments in aircraft. For example, A = 1.

A	B	C	D	E	G	H	I	J	L	M	N	O	P	R	S	T	U	W	Y
1	2	3	4	5	6	7	8	9	10	11	12	13	14	15	16	17	18	19	20

1. These brothers flew short flights in 1903, in North Carolina.

___ ___ ___ ___ ___ ___
19 15 8   6   7   17

2. This is what airlines were originally developed to carry.

___. ___.   ___ ___ ___ ___
18 16   11 1   8   10

3. Introduced in 1969, this plane can carry about 500 passengers.

___ ___ ___ ___ ___   ___ ___ ___
9   18 11 2   13   9   5   17

4. The Montgolfier brothers flew this over Paris in 1783.

___ ___ ___   ___ ___ ___   ___ ___ ___ ___ ___ ___ ___
7   13 17   1   8   15   2   1   10 10 13 13 12

5. He flew airmail on the Chicago-to-St. Louis route.

___ ___ ___ ___ ___ ___ ___   ___.
3   7   1   15 10 5   16   1

___ ___ ___ ___ ___ ___ ___ ___ ___
10 8   12 4   2   5   15 6   7

6. Henri Giffard flew this in 1852.

___ ___ ___ ___ ___ ___ ___ ___ ___
4   8   15 8   6   8   2   10 5

7. In 1936, the DC-3 set a record flying from Los Angeles to here.

___ ___ ___   ___ ___ ___ ___ ___ ___
12 5   19   9   5   15 16 5   20

8. Samuel P. Langley's airplane in 1896 was powered this way.

___ ___ ___ ___ ___   ___ ___ ___ ___ ___ ___ ___
16 17 5   1   11   14 13 19 5   15 5   4

9. This is what Boeing is developing to fly at 725 miles per hour.

___ ___ ___ ___ ___   ___ ___ ___ ___ ___ ___ ___
16 13 12 8   3   3   15 18 8   16 5   15

10. This type of airline service was launched in 1921.

___ ___ ___ ___ ___ ___ ___ ___ ___ ___ ___ ___ ___ ___ ___ ___
17 15 1   12 16 3   13 12 17 8   12 5   12 17 1   10

Find the names of famous people and aircraft, using the clues below.

1. It was the first successful passenger jet.

   B ____ ____ ____ ____ G   7 ____ 7

2. This plane will fly 725 miles per hour.

   S ____ N ____ ____   C ____ ____ ____ S ____ R

3. This is another name for the dirigible that Henry Giffard flew.

   ____ L ____ ____ P

4. This aircraft is powered by hot air.

   B ____ ____ ____ O ____ N

5. One of the most famous airliners to be developed, this can carry about 500 passengers.

   ____ O ____ ____ ____ G   ____ 4 ____

6. This airplane set a record flying from Los Angeles to New Jersey in 13 hours and four minutes.

   ____ C- ____

7. These Wright brothers flew the first manned airplane in 1903.

   O ____ ____ ____ L ____ ____   &   ____ I ____ B ____ R

8. He built a model plane that flew nearly a mile, unmanned.

   S ____ ____ ____ E ____   P.   ____ A ____ ____ L ____ Y

Write an appropriate question for each of the following answers. Use the question box for help in beginning your questions.

Question Box

- Who?
- What?
- Where?
- When?
- Why?
- How?

---

1. _____
   ➡ **Answer**: Boeing 707

2. _____
   ➡ **Answer**: Sonic Cruiser

3. _____
   ➡ **Answer**: Montgolfier brothers

4. _____
   ➡ **Answer**: Jumbo Jet

5. _____
   ➡ **Answer**: Samuel P. Langley

6. _____
   ➡ **Answer**: U.S. mail

7. _____
   ➡ **Answer**: Henri Giffard

8. _____
   ➡ **Answer**: DC-3

9. _____
   ➡ **Answer**: Charles A. Lindbergh

10. _____
   ➡ **Answer**: December 17, 1903

Answer the questions below and fill in the crossword.

Across

1. Spanish galleons had to have these on board for defense.

3. The Jahre Viking is longer than this building is tall.

6. In the 1500's, these ships hauled cargo around the world.

7. This was a wooden ship, built by the ancient Egyptians.

Down

1. These were the fastest ships of the era before steam.

2. This will be the world's biggest ship.

4. In 1818, these ships began taking passengers across the Atlantic.

5. Hauling this is a ship's most important job.

Use the code to answer the questions below. For example, B = 2.

A	B	C	D	E	F	G	H	I	J	L	M	N	O	P	R	S	T	U	W	Y
1	2	3	4	5	6	7	8	9	10	11	12	13	14	15	16	17	18	19	20	21

1. He was first to break the sound barrier.

___ ___ ___ ___ ___ ___
21   5   1   7   5   16

2. James Watt patented this in 1769.

___ ___ ___ ___ ___   ___ ___ ___ ___ ___ ___
17 18   5   1 12   5 13   7   9 13   5

3. The first wheels were made of this.

___ ___ ___ ___
20 14 14   4

4. He built the first Model T.

___ ___ ___ ___ ___   ___ ___ ___ ___
 8   5 13 16 21   6 14 16   4

5. People traveled in this in the 1730's.

___ ___ ___ ___ ___ ___ ___ ___ ___ ___
17 18   1   7   5   3 14   1   3   8

6. This allowed the Chinese to sail long distances.

___ ___ ___ ___ ___ ___ ___ ___   ___ ___ ___ ___ ___ ___ ___
12   1   7 13   5 18   8   3   3 14 12 15   1 17 17

7. Kirkpatric Macmillan invented this in Scotland.

___ ___ ___ ___ ___ ___ ___   ___ ___ ___ ___ ___ ___ ___
15   5   4   1 11   5   4   2   8   3 21   3 11   5

8. In 3500 B.C., Egyptians created these.

___ ___ ___ ___ ___ ___ ___ ___ ___
17   1   9 11   2 14   1 18 17

9. He broke the sound barrier on land.

___ ___ ___ ___   ___ ___ ___ ___ ___
 1 13   4 21   7 16   5   5 13

10. This was the first reusable spacecraft with a human crew.

___ ___ ___ ___ ___ ___ ___ ___
 3 14 11 19 12   2   9   1

Answer each clue with a word that contains double letters. Use the word bank for help.

1. In Mesopotamia, ancient people invented vehicles with these.

_____

2. This U.S. spacecraft landed on the moon.

_____

3. He piloted the first airplane on a 12-second flight.

_____

4. The Chinese invented this in 1100 B.C. to help them sail.

_____

5. This type of service began in 1830 on a steam train.

_____

6. He built the first car with an internal-combustion engine.

_____

7. This is the number of masts on Portuguese ships built in the 1450s.

_____

8. He broke the sound barrier on land, going 763 mph.

_____

9. Before sailboats, people in canoes did this with their hands.

_____

10. He patented the first successful steam engine.

_____

Word Bank

Andy Green	three	Orville Wright
magnetic compass	wheels	passenger rail
paddled	Apollo 11	Etienne Lenoir
	James Watt	

The names of important people in transportation have been split into two- or three-letter segments. The letters of the segments are in order, but the segments are scrambled. Put the pieces together to identify the personalities. Use the name bank below for help.

1. MES TT JA WA

_____

2. NRY RD HE FO

_____

3. RIN RI GA YU GA

_____

4. IG LLE WR OR HT VI

_____

5. AG LES YE CH ER AR

_____

6. LT BE FU RT ON RO

_____

7. DY EEN GR AN

_____

8. IR IEN NO NE ET LE

_____

9. NS GE EP ON GE ST HE OR

_____

10. TRI AN LL MA PA CK CMI RK KI

_____

Word Bank

Robert Fulton	Henry Ford	Charles Yeager
Yuri Gagarin	Kirkpatrick MacMillan	George Stephenson
James Watt	Orville Wright	Etienne Lenoir
	Andy Green	

Read these clues about important people in transportation. Write a name in each blank to complete the chart.

Location	Event/Achievement	Name
1. United States	first car manufacturing company	
2. Belgium	first car with internal-combustion engine	
3. United States	broke sound barrier	
4. France	flew first dirigible	
5. England	passenger rail service	
6. United States	assembly line for Model T	
7. Scotland	first pedaled bicycle	
8. United States	first gas-powered automobile	
9. Russia	orbited Earth in spaceship	
10. Germany	patented three-wheeled motor carriage	

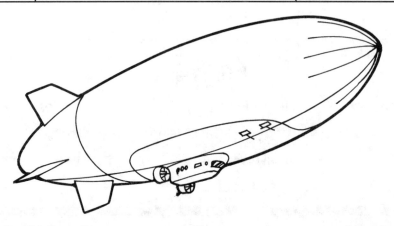

Answer Key

Page 10
1. Mount Kilimanjaro
2. Mount McKinley
3. Mount Kosciusko
4. Vinson Massif
5. Mount Elbrus
6. Mount Aconcagua
7. Mount Everest

Page 11

Page 12
1. Marco Polo
2. Christopher Columbus
3. Juan Ponce de Leon
4. James Cook
5. Francisco Pizarro
6. Bartolomeu Dias
7. Henry Hudson
8. Hernando Cortes

Page 13
1. Hernando de Soto
2. Ferdinand Magellan
3. Jacques Cartier
4. David Livingstone
5. James Cook
6. Vasco Nunez de Balboa
7. Marco Polo
8. Meriweather Lewis and William Clark
9. Leif Ericson
10. Francisco Pizarro

Page 14
1. Robert Cavelier
2. Hernando Cortes
3. Juan Ponce de Leon
4. Bartolomeu Dias
5. Christopher Colombos
6. Samuel de Champlain

7. Henry Hudson
8. Jacques Cartier
9. Francisco Pizarro
10. Ferdinand Magellan

Page 15
1. Magellan
2. Cortes
3. Hawaii
4. Cartier
5. de Soto
6. Balboa
7. Livingstone
8. Hudson
9. Ericson
10. Polo
11. Spain
12. France
13. Cook

Page 16
1. Oregon
2. Oklahoma
3. California
4. Montana or Wyoming
5. Colorado
6. Nevada
7. Oklahoma or New Mexico
8. Florida
9. Georgia
10. Kansas or Nebraska

Page 18
1. Lake City
2. U.S. highway
3. Moose Corners
4. County road
5. Lake City and Centerville
6. Lake City, Centerville, Mowmouth
7. U.S. highway
8. South

Page 19
1. South America
2. North Pole
3. North America
4. South America
5. North America
6. South Pole

Page 20
1. South
2. North
3. South
4. North
5. North
6. North
7. South
8. North

Page 21
1. North Pole
2. parallels
3. Equator
4. northern
5. hemispheres
6. South Pole
7. meridians
8. England

Page 22

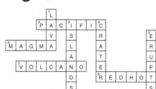

Page 23
1. Kelut
2. Mount Pelee
3. Tambora
4. Lake Nyos
5. Mt. Pinatubo
6. El Chichon
7. Mount Unzen
8. Krakatau
9. Mount Vesuvius
10. Mount St. Helens

Page 24
1. g
2. e
3. b
4. a
5. h
6. i
7. a
8. f
9. a
10. d
11. c

Page 25
1. Lake Nyos
2. Mount Vesuvius
3. Mount St. Helens
4. Krakatau or Krakatoa
5. Mount Unzen
6. El Chichon
7. Kelut
8. Mt. Pinatubo

Page 26
1. 5–6
2. 7–8
3. 0–2
4. 4–5
5. above 8
6. 6–7
7. 3–4
8. 2–3

Page 27
1. crust
2. California
3. fault
4. plate
5. earthquake
6. rock
7. moving
8. shakes

Page 28
1. earthquake
2. magnitude
3. crust
4. Richter Scale
5. plates
6. San Andreas
7. collide
8. fault

Page 36
1. Possible answers include Germany, Ghana, Grenada, Guinea, Guinea, Greece, Guyana, Guinea-Bissau, The Gambia, Gabon.

2. Lebanon
3. Canada
4. Algeria, Malaysia, Maldives, Mauritania, Pakistan, Singapore, Turkey, Uzbekistan
5. Somalia, Vietnam
6. Bangladesh, Japan, Panama
7. Zimbabwe
8. Australia, Fiji, New Zealand, Tuvalu.
9. Georgia
10. Possible choices are Antigua and Barbuda, Kazakhstan, Macedonia, Malaysia, Namibia.

Page 37

Answer: Australia

Page 38
1. h
2. c
3. e
4. b
5. a
6. i
7. d
8. f
9. g

Page 39
1. F
2. C
3. E
4. B
5. A
6. H
7. D
8. G

Page 40

Father	
Zeus	Jupiter
(Greek/Roman)	

Wife	
Hera	Juno
(Greek/Roman)	

Brother	
Poseidon	Neptune
(Greek/Roman)	

Brother	
Hades	Pluto
(Greek/Roman)	

Son	
Hephaestus	Vulcan
(Greek/Roman)	

Daughter	
Athena	Minerva
(Greek/Roman)	

Son	
Apollo	none
(Greek/Roman)	

Daughter	
Artemis	Diana
(Greek/Roman)	

Page 41
1. Middle East
2. Africa
3. Africa
4. Middle East
5. Middle East
6. Africa
7. Middle East
8. Africa
9. Africa
10. Middle East

Page 42
1. Jesus Christ
2. Nok culture
3. Alexander the Great
4. Ghana
5. pharaohs
6. Mesopotamia or southern Iraq
7. Kingdom of Axum
8. King David

Page 43
1. Alexander the Great
2. pharaohs
3. cuneiform
4. Moses
5. Code of Hammurabi
6. Jesus Christ
7. hieroglyphics
8. King David
9. Romans
10. Palestine
Riddle: Silent as a sphinx

Page 44
1. Nok Culture
2. Islam
3. Ghana
4. Kush
5. Iron
6. Axum
7. Bantu
8. Sub-Saharan Africans

Page 45
1. Kingdom of Kush—Major center of art, learning, and trade
2. Islamic religion—started in Africa and spread to Spain
3. Nok culture—strong in Nigeria. They used iron for tools and weapons
4. Sahara Desert—large part of African continent
5. Niger River—a river in Africa
6. Ethiopia—location of the Kingdom of Axum
7. West Africa—Bantu speaking peoples here began to move east and south
8. Ghana—first known African state south of the Sahara desert
9. ivory—traded widely in the Kingdom of Axum
10. Mediterranean Sea borders the northern part of Africa

Page 46
1. Shih Huang Ti
2. Chou peoples
3. Confucius
4. Chandragupta Maurya
5. Shang peoples
6. Siddhartha Gautama
7. Han peoples
8. Asoka
9. Ancient Chinese inventors
10. Hindu religion

Page 47
1. The Americas
2. The Americas
3. Ancient Europe
4. The Americas
5. Ancient Europe
6. Ancient Europe
7. The Americas
8. The Americas
9. Ancient Europe
10. The Americas

Page 48

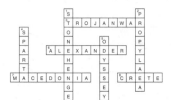

Page 49
1. Olympic Games
2. *Great Train Robbery*
3. Denton True Young
4. Tour de France
5. Mary Harris Jones
6. Comic Books
7. Helen Keller
8. Orville Wright

Page 50
1. Mary Harris Jones
2. Helen Keller
3. Tour de France
4. Denton True Young
5. *The Great Train Robbery*
6. Pierre and Marie Curie
7. Boston Pilgrims
8. Orville Wright

Page 57
1. i
2. a
3. d
4. j
5. f
6. b
7. c
8. g
9. e
10. h

Page 58
1. Polio vaccine
2. artificial heart
3. anesthesia
4. bifocal lenses

5. stethoscope
6. CAT scanner
7. insulin
8. X ray

Page 59
1. X-ray
2. anesthesia
3. bifocal lenses for glasses
4. fire extinguisher
5. airbag
6. smoke detector
7. CAT scan
8. penicillin
9. antibiotic for fungal diseases
10. lightning rod

Page 60
1. parachute
2. jet airplane
3. elevator
4. rollerblades
5. gasoline powered automobile
6. steam engine
7. motorcycle
8. Jet Ski
9. submarine
10. elevator, escalator, helicopter, jet airplane

Page 61
1. Gottlieb Daimler— These are inventors and their inventions.
2. United States— These are inventors and their countries.
3. steam locomotive— These are inventions and the dates on which they were invented.
4. helicopter—These are inventions and their inventors.
5. United States— These are inventors and their countries.
6. Scott Olson—These are inventors and their inventions.

7. propeller airplane— These are inventions and their inventors.
9. Germany—These are inventors and their countries.
10. Jesse W. Reno— These are inventors and their inventions.

Page 62
1. Samuel F.B. Morse
2. Alexander G. Bell
3. Sir Clive Sinclair
4. John Loud
5. Apple Computer
6. Ts'ai Lun
7. Chester Carlson
8. Nicholas Jacques Conte

Page 63
1. microscope
2. piano
3. X-ray
4. propeller airplane
5. automobile
6. typewriter
7. stethoscope
8. audiocassette
9. rocket engine
10. television

Page 64
1. eyeglasses
2. propeller
3. Reginald A. Fessenden
4. penicillin
5. word processor
6. Rene T.M.H. Laennec
7. ballpoint
8. rollerblades
9. Connaught Lab
10. cellular

Page 65
1. cellular phone
2. laptop computer
3. typewriter
4. paper
5. digital camera
6. telephone
7. computer
8. transistor radio

Page 66
1. compact disc
2. moving picture viewer
3. phonograph
4. videotape cassette
5. Walkman
6. motion picture projector
7. piano
8. steel tennis racket
9. portable camera
10. video game

Page 67
1. Gabriel D. Fahrenheit
2. Benjamin Franklin
3. Scott Olson
4. Sir Clive Sinclair
5. Clarence Birdseye
6. Elisha G. Otis
7. Robert H. Goddard
8. Sony

Page 68
1. rollerblades
2. steamboat
3. penicillin
4. typewriter
5. CAT Scanner

Page 69
1. frozen packaged food; Clarence Birdseye
2. Velcro; Georges de Mestral
3. windshield wipers; Mary Anderson
4. cash machine; Don Wetzel
5. refrigeration; Jacob Perkins
6. sewing machine; Elias Howe
7. vacuum cleaner; J. Murray Spangler
8. electric battery; Allesandro Volta
9. Post-its; 3M Company
10. air conditioning; Willis H. Carrier

Page 70
1. washing machine
2. electric light bulb
3. food processor
4. zipper
5. cylinder door lock
6. pop-top can
7. Polartec fabric or MET5 heat-generating jacket
8. lawn mower
9. dishwasher
10. cash machine

Page 71
1. space shuttle
2. telescope
3. magnifying glass
4. Aqua Lung
5. mercury thermometer
6. rocket engine
7. EZ-Rocket
8. cyclotron

Page 72
1. j	6. b
2. d	7. g
3. h	8. c
4. a	9. i
5. e	10. f

Page 79
1. Georgia
2. Apollo 11
3. Covered Wagon
4. Flying Cloud
5. Fossett
6. United States
7. hour
8. Express
9. Air Force
10. balloon
11. Concorde
12. Mayflower

Page 80

Answers will vary. The following are suggested responses.

2. Who sailed across the Atlantic in 2002 in 4 days, 17 hours, 28 minutes?
3. When did Apollo 11 take only four days to reach the moon?
4. Who flew from New York to Paris in the first nonstop flight across the Atlantic made by one person?
5. What was the name of the ship that took 66 days to sail across the Atlantic?
6. What pulled covered wagons across the United States?
7. How fast did the space shuttle *Columbia* fly?
8. What was the name of the balloon in which Betrand Piccard and Brian Jones flew around the world?
9. What flew coast-to-coast in 1 hour, 7 minutes, and 54 seconds at an average speed of 2,124 miles per hour?
10. What crossed the country by rail in 1876, taking 89 days and 8 hours?

Page 81

1. steam locomotive
2. Shinkansen
3. magnetic forces
4. electrified rail line
5. Tom Thumb
6. Acela Express
7. diesel engines
8. transcontinental railroad
9. bullet train
10. Train a Grande Vitesse

Page 82

1. three-wheeled motor carriage
2. Karl Benz
3. John W. Lambert
4. car manufacturing company
5. 1913
6. Ferdinand Porsche
7. Zero Emission Vehicles

Page 83

1. Henry Ford
2. hydrogen cells
3. Volkswagen "beetle"
4. aerodynamically designed
5. Global Positioning System
6. Germany
7. Massachusetts
8. affordable
9. fuel efficiency
10. electricity

Page 84

1. Henry Ford
2. Duryea Brothers
3. Gottlieb Daimler
4. Ferdinand Porsche
5. John W. Lambert
6. Karl Benz

Page 85

1. Wright
2. U.S. Mail
3. Jumbo Jet
4. hot air balloon
5. Charles A. Lindbergh
6. dirigible
7. New Jersey
8. steam-powered
9. Sonic Cruiser
10. transcontinental

Page 86

1. Boeing 707
2. Sonic Cruiser
3. blimp
4. balloon
5. Boeing 747
6. DC-3
7. Orville and Wilbur
8. Samuel P. Langley

Page 87

1. What was the first successful passenger jet?
2. What is the name of Boeing's new high-speed plane?
3. Who flew the first hot air balloon over Paris?
4. What was introduced in 1969 and can carry nearly 400 passengers?
5. Who built a model plane that flew a mile in 1896?
6. What were airlines originally developed to carry?
7. Who flew the first blimp?
8. What set a record flying from Los Angeles to New Jersey in 1936?
9. Who flew the Chicago-to-St. Louis route with the mail?
10. When did the Wright brothers make their first flight?

Page 88

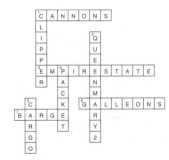

Page 89

1. Yeager
2. steam engine
3. wood
4. Henry Ford
5. stagecoach
6. magnetic compass
7. pedaled bicycle
8. sailboats
9. Andy Green
10. Columbia

Page 90

1. wheels
2. Apollo 11
3. Orville Wright
4. magnetic compass
5. passenger rail
6. Etienne Lenoir
7. three
8. Andy Green
9. paddled
10. James Watt

Page 91

1. James Watt
2. Henry Ford
3. Yuri Gagarin
4. Orville Wright
5. Charles Yeager
6. Robert Fulton
7. Andy Green
8. Etienne Lenoir
9. George Stephenson
10. Kirkpatrick MacMillan

Page 92

1. Duryea Brothers
2. Etienne Lenoir
3. Charles Yeager
4. Henri Giffard
5. George Stephenson
6. Henry Ford
7. Kirkpatrick MacMillan
8. John W. Lambert
9. Yuri Gagarin
10. Gottlieb Daimler